365

WITHDRAWN

Ways to a

SMARTER

PRESCHOOLER

CONTRIBUTING WRITERS:
Marilee Robin Burton
Susan G. MacDonald

CONSULTANT:
Susan Miller, Ph.D.

PUBLICATIONS INTERNATIONAL, LTD.

Contributing Writers:

Marilee Robin Burton is a freelance educational writer, consultant, and language arts specialist. She has ten years of experience as a teacher and has contributed to several publications, including *Early Childhood Workshop* and *Literary Place*. She is also the author and artist for several children's picture books and has a master of arts degree in early childhood education and human development.

Sharon G. MacDonald has a masters degree in education and has taught preschool and kindergarten level children for over 20 years. She has written numerous articles for *Pre-K Today* and *Early Childhood News*, and she wrote the book *Squish, Sort, Paint & Build*.

Consultant:

Susan Miller, Ph.D., is currently professor of early childhood education at the university level. She has written for over 150 journals, magazines, and books, including Scholastic's *Early Childhood Today*, *Childhood Education*, *Early Childhood News*, and the weekend activities for their *Parent & Child* magazine. Miller is a frequent presenter at the National Association for the Education of Young Children conferences and the Association of Childhood Education International Study conferences.

Front and back cover illustrations:
Kate Flanagan, George Ulrich

Illustrators: Kate Flanagan, George Ulrich

Louis Weber, CEO
Publications International, Ltd.
7373 North Cicero Avenue
Lincolnwood, Illinois 60712

Permission is never granted for commercial purposes.

Manufactured in U.S.A.

8 7 6 5 4 3 2 1

ISBN: 0-7853-4400-4

CONTENTS

Introduction 4

Chapter 1
My Amazing World—Exploring & Experimenting! 8

Chapter 2
It's All in My Head—Imagining & Pretending! 42

Chapter 3
See What I Can Make and Do—Creating & Playing! 72

Chapter 4
Using My Powers—Reflecting! 104

Chapter 5
Making My Brain Grow—Thinking & Expressing! 131

Chapter 6
What's All Around Me?—Observing & Listening! 150

Chapter 7
Between You and Me—Relating & Discussing! 176

Chapter 8
My Bouncy Body—Moving & Manipulating! 207

Index 236

INTRODUCTION

As your child explores the world, new ideas are stimulated. Inquisitive, your child becomes motivated to find out more, and so is challenged to experiment with manipulative materials, engage in exciting dialogues, create interesting inventions, and reflect on this newfound knowledge. In *365 Ways to a Smarter Preschooler,* you and your child will find wonderful, fun-filled activities to ignite the sparks of curiosity that will help build important skills that will make the child more knowledgeable about a vast array of concepts and processes.

This book is designed to be used with children from two to five years of age. As you read the directions, you will notice some activities can be undertaken independently, while others will require your assistance. Sometimes you help set up an activity, particularly if supervision for safety reasons is required.

Oftentimes, you may be involved as a play partner. You know your child best and therefore know best when he or she needs to be supervised. Small objects are called for in some projects, and some children (even four- and five-year-olds) still put things in their mouths. Always supervise your child carefully around small objects, balloons, etc. Also, supervise all children around water—no matter the age!

Some projects in this book call for paint or other materials that can be messy. Protect the child's clothing, if necessary, with a smock or apron. You may also want to protect the work surface with newspaper or a plastic table covering.

Adult help is needed for most of the activities in this book, but some activities can be done independently by the child. Some activities just need adult help for set-up, but after that the child can play without help from the adult. These symbols are next to each activity to guide you:

 Adult help is necessary for the activity.

 Child can do the activity independently.

  Adult help is needed for set-up; after that the child can do the activity independently.

Each activity has also been rated with a difficulty level: easy, medium, or challenging. The number of symbols will guide you:

 Activity is easy.

 Activity is of medium difficulty.

 Activity is challenging.

These ratings are simply a guide, however. Again, you know your child best. The activities should be fun and enough of a challenge that they will be exciting for the child. On the other hand, you do not want to frustrate your child with activities that are beyond him or her.

Children gain information in very different ways. Even though one medium activity may be easy for your child, another medium activity could be quite hard to do. If your child does not have prior experience with the topic, concept, or skills involved, even if he or she is older, the child may need to gain some basic skills or concepts first before moving along.

The chapters have a variety of themes to keep interest high. Feel free to skip around—your child's learning style may be visual and/or tactile, so he or she might really enjoy the activities in the chapter "My Amazing World—Exploring & Experimenting!" He or she

might be less motivated by the listening portion of "What's All Around Me—Observing & Listening!" Even if your child's learning style preference may not be auditory, this doesn't mean you should skip these activities, they just may not be his or her favorites. But it may prove more exciting than you expect!

In his book *Frames of Mind,* Howard Gardner describes various multiple intelligences that are present in all of us. If your child seems to learn best by classifying, and he or she likes to explore patterns and relationships, your child is probably a "logical/mathematical learner." Or, the child may learn best through rhythm, is good at picking up sounds, and likes to sing and play instruments. This child is most likely a "musical learner." While your child may have a preferred learning style and some intelligences may be stronger than others, it's possible to cultivate the other areas of intelligence. Encourage your child to try learning in different ways by trying a variety of the activities in this book from all the chapters. It's an intriguing, fun way to help raise a brighter, more interesting, well-rounded child.

Help your child gather the materials for the activities. Give him or her whatever support or time is needed. Provide places for the child to share his or her work with other family members. You may also want to consider using a camera or video recorder to document the work. Repeat favorite activities by adding a new twist. Let the child know that it's all right to take safe risks or to pull back if uncomfortable with any project. Most important, enjoy your time together as your child becomes intrigued, mystified, playful, and brighter!

Here's what's ahead for you:

CHAPTER 1 • MY AMAZING WORLD—EXPLORING & EXPERIMENTING!: Here the child uses all the senses as he or she is exposed to active learning. These hands-on activities will help develop scientific skills.

CHAPTER 2 ● IT'S ALL IN MY HEAD—IMAGINING & PRETENDING!: This chapter offers wonderful ways to develop self-expression through dramatic play, painting, storytelling, and more. It's a time to explore relationships.

CHAPTER 3 ● SEE WHAT I CAN MAKE AND DO—CREATING & PLAYING!: Here you will find lots of open-ended activities to encourage the child to explore freely. Creativity is brought to new heights while the child problem solves, dances, and builds.

CHAPTER 4 ● USING MY POWERS—REFLECTING!: The child has a chance to use a higher-level form of thinking. The child gathers his or her thoughts, analyzes them, and constructs meaning in very natural ways. The child develops problem-solving skills that will become necessary life-long skills.

CHAPTER 5 ● MAKING MY BRAIN GROW—THINKING & EXPRESSING!: Ideas germinate into potent thoughts in this chapter. Opportunities abound to translate these interesting thoughts into rich shared language.

CHAPTER 6 ● WHAT'S ALL AROUND ME—OBSERVING & LISTENING!: Quiet moments set the scene to see and hear what's happening. Listening activities enhance these seldom-taught skills, which are essential for daily safe living, as well as enjoyment of the child's surroundings.

CHAPTER 7 ● BETWEEN YOU AND ME—RELATING & DISCUSSING!: Chances to communicate with others raise your child to new levels of understanding. Here the child will have pressure-free opportunities to practice making messages clear.

CHAPTER 8 ● MY BOUNCY BODY—MOVING & MANIPULATING!: We know that young children learn best through hands-on experience. Exciting activities in this section encourage your child to develop not only big muscles, but little ones as well. This is a rich start toward refining the hand-eye coordination so necessary for later reading and writing successes.

As you and your child work and play, he or she will become more confident as new concepts are formed and skills are strengthened. Remember, the process is often more important than the product. Have a wonderful, pressure-free, exploratory time together!

MY AMAZING WORLD— EXPLORING & EXPERIMENTING!

Children are naturally curious, and they approach the world they live in with a sense of wonder. They are delighted to explore everything around them using hands, toes, eyes, ears, mouth, and nose! Children learn by looking, by tasting, by touching—by working directly with the everyday materials and experiences of their lives. Through active hands-on exploration they gain understanding and are able to construct knowledge. The activities in this chapter encourage the scientist in every young child, providing open-ended opportunities to investigate and learn about the everyday world.

DIRT DETECTIVE

There are amazing things to find in everyday dirt!

WHAT YOU'LL NEED: Trowel or small shovel, sieve or strainer, newspaper, dirt. Optional: Magnifying glass, paper, pencil

OBJECTIVE: Child will observe nature, and categorize and record observations.

The child can dig up a shovelful of dirt and spread it out onto newspaper. Have the child search through the dirt and look for rocks, pebbles, insects, seeds, roots, and other findings. Then sort the underground discoveries into categories. As an alternative to spreading out the dirt, the child can strain the dirt through a sieve or strainer to zero in on underground findings. To make the activity more advanced, the child can make a record of discoveries. The observations can be recorded through drawings or on a graph.

2 CATCHING RAINDROPS

Here's a way to catch a raindrop!

WHAT YOU'LL NEED: Bowl, measuring cup, flat tray, flour, salt, rain, fork, plate

OBJECTIVE: Child will observe and compare.

Raindrops fall so quickly it's never easy to see them individually or compare the size of one to another. The child can prepare a mixture in which to capture the falling raindrop shapes by mixing together 2 cups of flour and 1 cup of salt. The mixture is then spread out in a flat tray. The child should set the tray outside in the rain for a moment or two and then bring it back indoors. If there's no rain, the experiment can still be performed by gently dripping water from a wet hand over the mixture. Let the rain-catching mixture sit for a few hours. After that time, the flour and salt mixture will have created a mold around the shape the water made on impact. The shapes can be carefully scooped out with a fork and set on a plate in a warm place to harden. The child can then compare the sizes and shapes of the drops and ponder how and why hitting the ground makes them change. To extend this activity, encourage the child to repeat the experiment in different kinds of rain.

INVENTING AROMAS

Create personalized plant perfume!

 WHAT YOU'LL NEED: Wax paper, rolling pin, plant materials (onion, leaves, flower petals, lemon peel), strainer

OBJECTIVE: Child will use olfactory discrimination while watching the process of change.

The child can choose any of a variety of plants, flowers, fruits, or vegetables and try to capture their scents. Extract the aroma by placing pieces of one plant, fruit, or vegetable between two sheets of wax paper and then crushing them with a rolling pin. Place the crushed pieces inside a jar and add water to cover the pieces. Leave the jar overnight to allow the water to absorb the scent. After a day, with adult help, the child can pour the scented water through a strainer into a new jar, straining out the crushed pieces. Then test the fragrance. For a more advanced exploration, the child can create several scents. The strained,

scented water can be poured into jars and the child can use olfactory discrimination to figure out which scent is which, or each fragrance can be poured into two jars so the child can try to match the scents that are the same.

REFLECTING RAINBOWS

4

A mirror can create a magical rainbow!

WHAT YOU'LL NEED: Small, unbreakable mirror, glass of water

OBJECTIVE: Child will observe light refraction while experimenting with light reflection.

Creating rainbows and dancing them around the room is magical as well as scientific. With adult supervision, the child can create a rainbow with a small mirror and a clear glass of water. Have the child carefully place the glass of water in direct sunlight and then submerge a small mirror halfway in the water (half of mirror is below and half is above water line). By tilting and rotating the mirror the child will catch the sunlight, which will then be refracted through the water to create the rainbow colors.

5

MUD PAINTING

Mud painting is messy, but oh so much fun!

WHAT YOU'LL NEED: Plastic containers, dirt, water, paper, cardboard, foil, large and small brushes

OBJECTIVE: Child will experiment and use problem-solving skills.

Can you paint with mud? The child can experiment with muddy mixtures to answer this question and also to determine what consistency of mud paints best. Let the child mix dirt and water in plastic containers to different consistencies, then experiment with mud painting. The child can also explore painting with different kinds of brushes and on different kinds of surfaces.

FLOATING BOATING

Can you make a boat that floats?

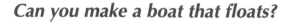

WHAT YOU'LL NEED: Aluminum foil, tub or sink, water. Optional: Buttons, paper clips, or pennies; modeling clay; paper; crayons

OBJECTIVE: Child will use creative problem-solving skills, while predicting and experimenting.

What shape works best when building a boat? What shapes don't work? Why? These are questions the child can tackle while creating boat shapes out of common materials. The child can experiment with aluminum-foil boat building by bending, folding, scrunching, and crumpling the foil. Boats can be tested in a plastic tub or sink filled with water. After a shape has been created that successfully floats, the experiment can be taken one step further. The child can test out how much weight a boat can carry before sinking. Pennies, paper clips, or buttons can be used for weights. The child can add one item at a time, keeping track of how many it takes to sink a boat. The number can be recorded using crayons to color in squares in a bar graph. The difficulty of the activity can be increased even further by inviting the child to create floating boat shapes using modeling clay. (Always supervise children around water and when they handle small objects, which could be choking hazards.)

WHAT PAINTS HOW?

Discover what shapes do to paint!

 WHAT YOU'LL NEED: Feather, twig, leaf, cotton ball, cotton swab, sponge, paint, paper, variety of brushes

OBJECTIVE: Child will use observation skills through exploration and comparison.

Here's an artistic way for the child to experiment with a variety of improvised paint tools and have fun noticing the different results that can be achieved using them. Provide the child with a wide variety of paint tools, both traditional and improvised. The child can then explore and experiment with the tools provided and draw conclusions about how different tools paint. To make more difficult, include the child when you choose the tools to be used, and continue to add new implements for further testing. To simplify, allow the child to experiment with only two or three very different kinds of implements at a time.

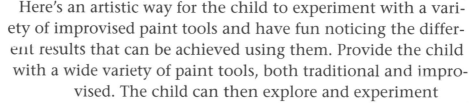

Let early education be a sort of amusement; you will then be better able to discover the child's natural bent.

Plato

WHO FITS WHAT?

8

▼▼▼▼▼▼▼▼▼▼▼▼▼▼▼▼▼▼▼▼▼▼▼▼▼▼▼

Big, little, medium—which jar fits which lid?

 WHAT YOU'LL NEED: Assorted plastic jars and screw-on lids

OBJECTIVE: Child will predict, compare, and test out size relationships.

Jars and lids come in a very large variety of sizes, colors, and shapes. It can be quite a challenge to find all the right tops to all the right bottoms when everything has been un-screwed and undone! The adult can provide a large assortment of jars and lids for the task and then challenge the child to find the correct top for each empty bottom!

9

MELTDOWN

▼▼▼▼▼▼▼▼▼▼▼▼▼▼▼▼▼▼▼▼▼▼▼▼▼▼▼

How fast will ice melt? Let's find out!

 **WHAT YOU'LL NEED:** Ice cubes, small self-sealing bags

OBJECTIVE: Child will use scientific skills to predict, test, observe, ponder, and draw conclusions.

Here's an activity that will help the child discover what it takes to melt objects: heat! The child can place the same number of ice cubes into four self-sealing bags and then carefully seal each bag. The child can then choose a different part of the room or house to place each bag. One can be put in a sunny window, one near a radiator, one in the refrigerator, and one can be held between two warm palms! Have the child predict which cubes will melt the quickest and which the slowest—then observe the results.

BLOWING BEAUTIFUL BUBBLES

Everyone loves blowing bubbles—blow away!

WHAT YOU'LL NEED: Tub, bubble solution (8 tablespoons liquid detergent, 1 quart water, 1 tablespoon glycerin), bubble wand, berry basket, can with both ends removed, cardboard tubes, six-pack plastic rings, plastic straw, coated wire clothes hanger. Optional: Pipe cleaners

OBJECTIVE: Child will experiment and use problem-solving skills.

Bubble making is a delight to both the artistic and the scientific temperaments of a child. The child can experiment with different tools and seek to discover what makes the best bubbles and why. The child can explore which tool makes the biggest bubble, the smallest bubble, the longest bubble, the strongest bubble, the most bubbles, and even the prettiest bubble! To make the activity more difficult, invite the child to make bubble wands in different shapes using pipe cleaners to observe, compare, and draw conclusions about the bubbles.

Youth is wholly experimental.
Robert Louis Stevenson

BUMPING, BOUNCING BALLS

11

Not just for sport, balls are also learning tools!

WHAT YOU'LL NEED: Variety of balls such as tennis ball, Ping-Pong ball, foam ball, football, rubber ball

OBJECTIVE: Child will gain experience and practice making predictions and testing them out.

Bouncing balls are not only fun for games and sports, they can be wonderful scientific tools as well. The child can gather a bunch of balls together and make a variety of predictions about them. Predictions can include which balls will bounce and which won't, which balls can be tossed the highest, which balls can be thrown or rolled the farthest, and which balls will float or sink. Encourage the child to make one kind of prediction at a time and then test out that prediction on all the balls. For a further puzzler, invite the child to think about what happens when a ball loses its air. If a flat ball is available, have the child test that out, too!

12

SOAPY SIMILARITIES

Different kinds of soap are all good for cleaning, but are they all the same?

WHAT YOU'LL NEED: Different types of soap (bar soap, liquid detergent, soap flakes), plastic containers filled with water (one for each type of soap), spoon, eggbeater

OBJECTIVE: Child will make comparisons and draw conclusions.

Gather up several different kinds of soaps. Invite the child to play! Then think up categories in which to compare the soaps and test out how they measure up. Some things the child might test are: Which soap makes the most bubbles in water? Which will float in water? Which dissolves the best? Which is the most slippery? Which washes hands best?

SOCK WALK

Go searching for seeds without looking for them!

WHAT YOU'LL NEED: Large pair of old socks, newspaper, plant pot or jar, soil, water.
Optional: Magnifying glass, plastic bag, rubber band

OBJECTIVE: The child will observe, experiment, and draw conclusions.

Invite the child to put on an old pair of socks on top of his or her shoes. Then take a walk together in the yard, a garden area, or a local park. After returning home, the child can take off the socks and lay them on a newspaper and carefully look over all the odds and ends that have stuck to the socks. There may be some seeds stuck to the socks! Cover the work area with newspaper. Invite the child to prepare a planting pot for the seeds by filling a pot or jar with soil. The child can plant everything that looks like it might be a seed in the pot by poking holes in the soil, inserting the seeds, and then gently covering them with soil. Have the child place the pot in a sunny place, add a little water, and watch to see what grows.

(What grows will depend on the season.) To help the seeds germinate, the child can create a greenhouse by covering the pot with a plastic bag and sealing it with a rubber band.

14 COOKED AND UNCOOKED

Hard, soft, mashed, or crunchy—
does it affect the taste of food?

WHAT YOU'LL NEED: Apples, vegetable peeler, plastic knife, pot, potato masher, bowl, spoon

OBJECTIVE: The child will predict, compare, and observe change.

Take a taste test using only one food by making some changes in how the food is prepared. Does cooking change the flavor? Does size or shape make a fruit taste different? Does a shredded vegetable taste the same as an uncut vegetable? The child can make predictions and then test them out. Have everyone wash hands! Peel and core the apple. With adult supervision, invite the child to help cut up the apple into small pieces. The child can then put the pieces into a pot. Cook the apple slowly until it is mushy. While the apple is cooking, the child can cut a second apple into slices to be eaten raw. After the cooked apple has become mushy, the child can mash it by using a potato masher. The fresh applesauce can then be scooped into a bowl, tasted, and compared to the raw apple slices. Encourage the child to describe the differences, including how each one tastes. To make the activity more difficult, you can also include any of the following in the test: grated apples, uncooked applesauce, or fresh apple juice. For uncooked applesauce, put apple slices in the blender and blend with a little bit of water. Another way to make the activity more difficult is by making other cooked and uncooked comparisons. For a variation, use carrots. They can be diced, sliced, curled, shredded, cut in sticks, or eaten whole. They can be steamed in chunks. They can be cooked with a little water and then mashed or pureed. They can be juiced!

Knowledge is power.
Francis Bacon

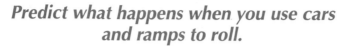

ROLLING, ROLLING, ROLLING

*Predict what happens when you use cars
and ramps to roll.*

 WHAT YOU'LL NEED: Block or shoe box, cardboard, masking tape, paper, toy cars, marbles, cylinder blocks, crayons

OBJECTIVE: Child will predict, test, and draw conclusions.

The child can create a ramp by setting one end of a piece of cardboard on a shoe box or block and the other end on the floor. To make the ramp more secure, the child can tape the two pieces together. Invite the child to gather a group of toy cars and other round or rolling toys to test. The child can guess which will roll the farthest and make guesses as to how far each will roll. A large piece of paper (even newspaper will do) set in front of the ramp can be used to record both guesses and actual roll distances. Predictions can be marked on the paper with one color crayon and results can be marked in a different color.

DOES IT DISSOLVE?

16

Become a scientist to find out what dissolves!

 WHAT YOU'LL NEED: Water containers, spoon, variety of objects (salt, pepper, sugar, pebbles, ice cubes, laundry detergent, polystyrene foam, oil, marbles, lima beans)

OBJECTIVE: Child will explore and observe the properties of different materials.

Invite the child to be a scientist and make predictions about what substances can be dissolved in water. Then experiment to find out if your predictions are correct. Gather materials together with the child. Start by adding sugar to the water to show the child what dissolve means. The child can then examine each item, look at it, touch it, and predict whether or not it will dissolve in water. The child can then test the items, one by one!

MINGLE & MERGE COLOR SPLURGE

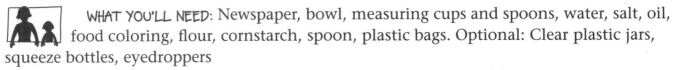

Watching colors change is fun!

 **WHAT YOU'LL NEED:** Newspaper, bowl, measuring cups and spoons, water, salt, oil, food coloring, flour, cornstarch, spoon, plastic bags. Optional: Clear plastic jars, squeeze bottles, eyedroppers

OBJECTIVE: Child will predict, explore, experiment, and observe.

Color mixing can be fascinating to observe, but when mushing and mixing playdough is part of the process, it is doubly enticing. Cover the work surface with newspaper. Make three balls of playdough in the primary colors (red, blue, and yellow) as a base for mixing experiments. Invite the child to help make the dough. For each ball, mix together ½ cup cold water, ½ cup salt, 1 teaspoon oil, and food coloring. Then gradually mix in 1½ cups flour and 1 teaspoon cornstarch until a dough forms. Knead the dough into a malleable ball. After the three balls are made, the child can experiment by mixing portions of the different colors together to see the results. To add challenge, encourage the child to make as many different colors out of the three original balls as possible. The child can then classify and group all the colors created or arrange them in a series! A simpler variation is coloring water with food color to make red, blue, and yellow water that the child can mix. The colored water can be placed in plastic squeeze bottles and the child can squeeze combinations of colors into clear jars, or the water can be put into jars and the child can use eyedroppers to mix the colors into new jars.

PAPER CAPER

18

▼▼▼▼▼▼▼▼▼▼▼▼▼▼▼▼▼▼▼▼▼▼▼▼▼▼▼▼▼▼▼▼▼

Paper is very light, but how far will it go if you blow?

WHAT YOU'LL NEED: Several index cards or small pieces of paper (all the same size and kind), block or book

OBJECTIVE: Child will gain experience making predictions and testing hypotheses.

Challenge the child to estimate how far a small paper can be blown. The child can place a block or book on the floor to mark the estimate and then test the estimate by putting the card on the floor and sending it off with a large puff of air. The child can mark the actual length it moved and retest to see if the results are always the same. Encourage the child to think of ways to alter the paper to change the results. What happens if the paper is folded? Or crumpled? Are the results the same? Different? Why?

19

DECAY AWAY

● ●

Don't throw it away! Observe it!

WHAT YOU'LL NEED: Banana peel, self-sealing plastic bag

OBJECTIVE: Child will observe the stages of natural aging and decay.

The child will enjoy watching what happens and commenting on the natural decay of what we usually throw away. The child can save a banana peel after a banana snack. Have the child put the peel into a self-sealing plastic bag and then carefully seal the bag. The bag can be placed on a sunny windowsill where its decomposition can be safely observed for several weeks. If possible, hang the bag in front of the window with a clothespin for even better viewing! Encourage the child to report and describe the changes seen in the banana peel from day to day.

20

SOUNDING OFF

Make lots of noise—all with your parents' approval.

WHAT YOU'LL NEED: Variety of containers with tops (coffee can, film canister, empty oatmeal box, empty margarine tub), variety of fillers (paper clips, buttons, uncooked rice, salt, uncooked kidney beans)

OBJECTIVE: Child will enhance auditory discrimination by listening carefully.

Sounding off and exploring noise-making is natural to a young child, but listening takes practice and skill! The child can experiment with sounds by putting different kinds of materials in varying amounts into differently shaped containers and then closing them, shaking them, and listening! To simplify the activity, decrease the variables. The child can use all the same size and shape of container and fill them with different materials or fill differently sized and shaped containers with varying amounts of the same material. To increase the difficulty, invite the child to line the containers up in order from the softest noise-maker to the loudest. (Supervise young children; small objects can be choking hazards.)

I am never afraid of what I know.
Anna Sewell

READ MY BREEZEOMETER

21

My breezeometer will show how the wind blows!

WHAT YOU'LL NEED: Dowel or stick, yarn, scissors, cardboard, paper, pencil, plastic lid, fabric scrap, washer, tape

OBJECTIVE: Child will learn to observe and measure changes.

It's easy to look out the window and notice whether the wind is blowing or to stand outside and comment on the breeze, but it's not as easy to compare one day's breeze to another day's wind. Here's a useful tool to help the child compare a light breeze to a heavier wind. Start by locating a long dowel or have the child find a long stick outdoors to use as the breezeometer base. Then gather together a variety of small items of varying weights and ask the child to arrange them from light to heavy. With adult help, the child can attach the items to the stick (in weight order, with lightest at the top) by taping a piece of yarn to each item and then tying the yarn pieces to the stick, leaving each item dangling a few inches. The items should be tied at intervals of a few inches apart. Now the breezeometer is ready to test the wind! Take the stick outside and plant it in the ground so that it stands upright. The breezeometer can be used to gauge the wind strength by observing which items blow in a breeze. In a very mild breeze only the lightest items will blow and the heavy ones will remain hanging. A medium breeze will blow the light and medium-light items. In a strong wind, everything will blow!

FROZEN ART

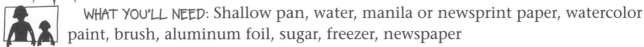

Here's a new way to explore ice . . . paint on it!

 WHAT YOU'LL NEED: Shallow pan, water, manila or newsprint paper, watercolor paint, brush, aluminum foil, sugar, freezer, newspaper

OBJECTIVE: Child will observe properties of water and how it can change.

The child can create frozen paper by dipping a piece of absorbent paper into a shallow pan of water. The child then places the wet paper onto a sheet of aluminum foil the same size and puts a second sheet of foil on top of the wet paper. Place the paper and foil in the freezer until frozen. Then take it from the freezer and peel off both sheets of foil. Now it's time to paint! When the picture is finished, have the child sprinkle it with sugar to create a textured effect. Then place the picture in the freezer to freeze the paint! (No foil is needed this time.) When frozen, the paper is removed from the freezer and placed on newspaper to dry.

INVITE A BUG HOME

Make a bug home so you can bring a bug home!

WHAT YOU'LL NEED: Plastic cup, plastic spoon, nylon stocking foot, twist tie

OBJECTIVE: Child will make observations about the natural world.

Gather up the materials with the child and take them outdoors. The child can scoop some dirt into the cup, and then add a rock or pebbles, a twig, and a leaf to make a bug house. Add a spoonful of water for moisture. After the house is "furnished," the child slips the house inside the stocking. The child scoops the bug inside the cup and closes the stocking top with the twist tie. Observe the bug for an afternoon before setting it free.

MAKE A MAGNET

24

*Attraction is fun when you investigate
and explore with magnets!*

WHAT YOU'LL NEED: Magnet, iron nail (not galvanized), a variety of magnetic and nonmagnetic items (paper clip, button, penny, washer, screw, cotton ball, eraser, feather, brass fastener)

OBJECTIVE: Child will make predictions, comparisons, and classify items.

Invite the child to experiment with the magnet and see what it will pick up; then have the child try to pick up objects with the nail. The child can magnetize an iron nail and experiment again. Magnetize the nail by stroking it with the strong magnet 50 to 100 times. The strokes all need to be in one direction!

25

HOW MANY WILL FIT?

1, 2, 3—How many can there be?

WHAT YOU'LL NEED: Small clear plastic jar, collection of the same kind of items (walnuts in the shell, small wooden cubes, or marbles)

OBJECTIVE: Child will practice estimating and counting to develop number sense.

It's traditional to look at a group of items and estimate how many there are. Here's a backward way to estimate! Invite the child to look at a small container and a group of objects and estimate how many of the objects will fit inside the container! The child can then check the estimation by counting the objects while placing them inside. For easy estimating use a small clear jar and objects large enough so that only five to ten will fit inside. To increase the difficulty use larger jars and smaller items!

26

BE STILL AND SMELL!

With this little nose I smell . . . ?

WHAT YOU'LL NEED: Variety of spices (garlic, cinnamon, nutmeg, oregano), stiff paper squares, rubber cement, hole punch, self-sealing plastic bags

OBJECTIVE: Child will use olfactory discrimination.

Make spice cards together with the child by spreading rubber cement on a paper square and sprinkling it with a spice. Make two cards for each kind of spice. When the cards have dried, punch several holes in each one so fragrances will waft through for easy smelling when upside down. (Be sure cement has dried before child smells the cards.) The child can turn all the cards upside down, mix them up, and try to match mates. Encourage the child to pick up cards and sniff them, keeping the cards face down while doing so! For easier sorting, the child can turn over all the cards and use visual cues to help make the matches. Spice cards should be kept in self-sealing plastic bags, one kind of spice per bag, when they are not being used.

It is the mind that makes the body.
Sojourner Truth

WATER MELODIES

Everyone loves a beautiful melody!

 WHAT YOU'LL NEED: Glasses and jars, water, spoon, tub, water pitcher

OBJECTIVE: Child will explore and seriate sounds to fine-tune auditory discrimination.

Here's a simple way to create pretty sounds in which the child can explore both altering the sound of each instrument as well as creating personal tunes. With adult supervision, the child can place glasses in a plastic tub and fill them with different amounts of water. The child can then gently tap the glasses with a spoon to make sounds. The sound of each jar or glass can be modified by adding more water with the water pitcher or pouring some water out. To make this more difficult, the child can order the glasses according to the sound scale from the highest pitch to the lowest. If the glasses are different sizes and shapes, the child will need to rely fully on listening skills in order to complete this task. To simplify, fewer glasses that are all of the same size and shape can be used. For an added challenge, ask the child to figure out how much water to add to two differently shaped glasses in order to get the same sound when each one is tapped.

PUDDLE TESTING

Puddles disappear—let's find out how!

WHAT YOU'LL NEED: Puddle after a rainy day, chalk. Optional: Old plate, wax pencil

OBJECTIVE: Child will make predictions, measurements, observations, and draw conclusions.

Rain is mysterious. It falls out of the sky; then it disappears. How does it happen? The child can begin to make sense of some of nature's mysteries through careful observation. Here is simple activity for a puddle study. Invite the child to find a puddle on a cement area on a sunny day after a rainfall. The child can then draw a chalk line around the puddle right at the water's edge. Ask the child to predict what might happen to the puddle now that the rain has stopped. Will it dry? How fast? Return to the puddle with the child several times during the day to check and see what has happened. If it is still there but has gotten smaller, the child can draw a new chalk border. Encourage the child to think about where the water went and what helped it dry up. As a variation, the child can take an old plate outside on a sunny day and pour water into it to create a puddle. The child can mark the puddle on the plate with a wax pencil to record the evaporation.

29 MAKE PAPER

Use old paper to make new!

WHAT YOU'LL NEED: Paper towels, bowl, hot water, powdered starch, tablespoon, eggbeater, shallow pan, screen, newspaper, rolling pin. Optional: Colored tissue paper, glitter, leaf pieces, flower pieces, ribbon, dryer lint, small flowers, coffee grounds, embroidery floss cut in small pieces

OBJECTIVE: Child will participate in and observe the process of transformation and also that of material recycling.

Paper is not made just from trees. It's easy and interesting to create new paper from old paper! Invite the child to tear up several paper towels into small pieces and put them in a large bowl. Cover the towel pieces with hot water and add a table-spoon of starch. With adult supervision the child can beat up the mixture until it turns to mush and then pour the mush into the shallow pan. The screen is slid into the bottom of the pan and the child "mashes the mush" around to cover the screen! The child can then lift the screen and allow some of the water to drip out back into the pan before setting the screen down on a stack of newspapers. The child can put more newspaper on top and use a rolling pin to squeeze out more water. Remove the newspaper on top and gently lift the paper off the screen and set on dry newspaper to dry fully. For a variation, col-ored tissue paper can be added to the paper mix before blending to make colored paper. After the paper has been blended to mush, try adding glitter, leaf pieces, ribbon, flow-ers, or the other optional materials mentioned in What You'll Need, for unusual papers. Spices can also be added to make fragrant papers. If the child really enjoys this activity, extend the activity by having the child experiment using different kinds of paper for the original torn paper base. Try paper bags, notebook paper, holiday cards, newspaper, Sunday funnies, and any other paper you think would be interesting—then observe the results.

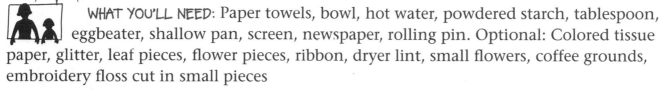

SEEDS, ROOTS, AND SHOOTS

Besides seeds, what else will grow?

WHAT YOU'LL NEED: Lima bean, sweet potato, carrot top, plant cutting, jars, soil, toothpicks, water

OBJECTIVE: Child will experiment to explore, observe, and draw conclusions.

Planting seeds isn't the only way to grow plants. New plants can also grow from roots, tubers, leaves, and stems. For many plants this is a form of self-preservation, in case their seeds cannot sprout because of conditions in the natural environment. Invite the child to experiment with different forms of plant growth! A lima bean can be planted in a glass jar. With adult supervision, the child can fill a glass jar with soil and push several beans down inside the jar along the edge. The child can watch the sprouting and growth of roots. Set the jar in a sunny place and keep the soil moist. For sweet potato growth, the child can pierce the sweet potato with three or four toothpicks around its middle and set it in a jar so the toothpicks sit on the edge and the rounded end of the potato peeks out of the jar. The sweet potato should be placed in the jar, narrow side down. The child can add water to the jar nearly to the top and set that jar in a sunny place also. For potato growth, the child can prepare the potato in the same way as the sweet potato, making sure to place the potato with the "eyes" on top. To grow a carrot plant, the child can cut off the top of a carrot and set it in a jar and cover it to the top of the carrot with water. Set the carrot in a sunny place too! Leaves cut from plants, such as philodendrons, set in water, will sprout new roots and can then be replanted in a pot of soil to grow a new plant.

Education is seeing things in the working.
Thomas Alva Edison

SOAK IT TO ME

What soaks in and what won't?

WHAT YOU'LL NEED: Eyedropper, cup of water, paper towel, cardboard, polystyrene foam, cork, sponge, wax paper, cotton ball, plastic spoon, aluminum foil, button, eraser, rock

OBJECTIVE: Child will use critical thinking to draw conclusions.

The child can make predictions about which items will absorb water and then test them by using an eyedropper to drip water on them. Have the child drip water on the paper towel first to show what absorb means. Then have the child drip water on the other items listed above. After testing, the child can sort the objects into categories and describe the discoveries.

EXPLORE THE DARK

What does the dark look like?

WHAT YOU'LL NEED: Flashlight

OBJECTIVE: Child will experiment, observe, and describe some properties of light.

If you turn on the light, can you see the dark? Do things look different in the dark and in the light? Answer these questions and more. The child can use a flashlight to explore the dark. Encourage the child to turn the light on and off, to notice how objects look in the dark and in the light, to explore the light trail the light makes, and to talk about and describe all that is seen and unseen! Then play a game of follow the leader with light. Take turns shining the beam around the room, inviting the other person to "follow the light!" Another variation is light tag. One person moves the beam around, if the other can tag the beam, the flashlight changes hands.

DIP AND DYE

Fold, dip, and dye to make pretty paper!

 WHAT YOU'LL NEED: Six-sectioned muffin tin, plastic pitcher, water, food coloring, paper towels, newspaper

OBJECTIVE: Child will experiment with color mixing and symmetrical design.

 With a few simple ingredients the child will transform white paper towels into decorative works of art! Have the child fill each section of a muffin tin halfway with water using a plastic pitcher. With adult help, the child can add a few drops of food coloring to each section to make different colors. The child then folds a paper towel into small squares or triangles and dips each corner into a different color. The paper towel is then unfolded and laid on the newspaper to dry.

COLORFUL MELTDOWN

Painting with ice is cool!

 WHAT YOU'LL NEED: Water, ice cube tray, food coloring, freezer, paper. Optional: Paper towel, pan or newspaper

OBJECTIVE: Child will experience the changing properties of water as well as color mixing.

To create ice paints, the child can fill an ice tray with water and add a few drops of food coloring to each section; the adult may need to help. Then put the tray in the freezer. After the cubes have frozen, the child can use the cubes to draw, holding one cube at a time and drawing slowly so the heat from the child's hand melts the cube. As the child uses different cubes, the colors will blend. For a variation, the child can place two or three colored cubes on a paper towel in a pan or on newspapers. Watch the colors mix as the cubes melt.

PAINTING WITH NATURE

Make your own paints—with nature!

WHAT YOU'LL NEED: Fruits or vegetables and other natural items (beets, blueberries, purple cabbage, spinach, red onion skins, walnut shells, coffee grounds, marigold or dandelion flowers), water, pots, pot holder, brush, paper, white cotton twine, scissors, newspaper. Optional: Nontoxic white glue

OBJECTIVE: Child will explore creating as well as transforming nature items into products with other uses.

Paints in a multitude of colors are easily available at any local art store, but what did people do before they could buy paints at the store? They made their own! Make natural dyes by simmering beets, berries, onion skins, or the other items listed above until the water turns color. Then reserve the water, and let it cool. (The vegetables can be saved for soups, the fruit for pudding, and the onion skins tossed away!) The child can help with the cooking by placing the items in the pot (one fruit or vegetable per pot) and adding the water. With the child, check the water every five minutes to determine when the dye is ready. After the colored water has cooled, the child can use it to paint on paper or to dye cotton twine. To dye the twine, let it soak in the vegetable dye for an hour, and then set it to dry on newspaper. As a further activity, the child can make several colors of twine and then use the naturally dyed twine for a collage.

Imagination is more important than knowledge.
Albert Einstein

36 HOW DOES MY SHADOW GROW?

Sunny days make great shadows—at noon, 1:00, and 2:00!

 WHAT YOU'LL NEED: Paper, crayons, chalk. Optional: Teddy bear or other toy, coffee can, stick, stones or soil

OBJECTIVE: Child will make observations and draw conclusions.

Sunny days and shadows are a perfect combination for outside investigation and experimentation! Go outside together on a sunny day and look for shadows. The child can make shadow records by placing paper on the ground on top of intriguing shadow shapes and tracing the shapes with a crayon or tracing the shapes on cement with chalk. The adult can hold the paper down while the child draws. To add to the shadow exploration, the child can observe and record morning, noon, and dusk shadows. Find a sunny place on the pavement and take turns tracing each other's shadows in the morning. Trace around where feet are placed so you can each step into the same position the next time you measure. Come back and retrace both shadows at lunchtime, and again in the afternoon. How are the shadows different? How did they change? For a variation, the child could place a teddy bear or a toy in the sun and trace the changing shadows during the day. Or to create a simple shadow to trace, the child can put a tall stick or ruler in a coffee can filled with soil or stones.

PLANT MAZE

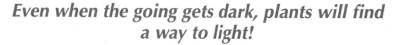

Even when the going gets dark, plants will find a way to light!

WHAT YOU'LL NEED: Lima beans, small planting pot, soil, small cardboard box or large shoe box, cardboard

OBJECTIVE: Child will learn about phototropism, observe nature, and draw conclusions.

Plants always grow toward sunlight (phototropism). Here's an activity for the child to test a plant's determination to find the light. The child can fill a small pot with soil and plant two or three lima beans in the soil an inch or so deep. The child can place the pot in a sunny place, water the soil, and keep it moist until the beans begin to grow and sprout. After the plant has begun to peek above the soil, the child can place it inside a plant maze. Help the child create the maze by cutting a hole (approximately 3 inches in diameter) in one side of the box. Cut two pieces of cardboard to fit inside the box, making two walls. Cut a hole in each wall on opposite sides. Place the walls inside the box. When the maze is ready and the plant has sprouted, the child can place the plant in the box in the section farthest away from the outside hole. Let the child close or cover the box. Place the plant maze in a sunny place, and check the plant regularly to keep it moist. Within days the plant will find a way through the maze and out to the light! To add to this activity, the child can grow two lima bean plants in full sunlight. After the plant has leafed out, the child can cover two or three of the leaves with aluminum foil for a week so that they do not receive sunlight. Watch what happens!

Huntington City
Township Public Library
255 West Park Drive
Huntington, IN 46750

RAIN PAINTING

38

Can rain paint? It can with a little help from a child!

WHAT YOU'LL NEED: Powdered tempera paint, sprinkle jars, paper

OBJECTIVE: Child will participate in and observe color mixing and the process of change.

Invite the child (with supervision) to sprinkle a few colors of powdered tempera paint on paper. It's time to let the rain create a picture with the paints. (Adults should be careful that children do not inhale paint powder.) The child can set the paper outside on the ground on a drizzly day, weighing down each corner with a rock and leaving it outside for a few minutes. If the rain is more than a drizzle, the child (with a raincoat and rain hat on!) can stand in the rain and hold the paper for a moment or two before bringing it back indoors to dry.

39

BUG BANQUET

Feed the bugs—maybe they like chocolate, too!

WHAT YOU'LL NEED: Sugar, salt, oatmeal, cracker crumbs, potato peel, cheese

OBJECTIVE: Child will make predictions, observations, and draw conclusions.

Most everyone knows the favorite foods of people and some animals, but what do bugs eat? The child can perform an experiment to find bugs' culinary delights. Invite the child to make predictions about food bugs might like. The child can then place small amounts of food outside (not too close to the house!) where the child has seen bugs. The bugs may need time to find the food, so check several times during the day to see what happens.

GOOD GREEN GROWTH

What do plants need—are sun and water necessary?

WHAT YOU'LL NEED: Four plastic cups, potting soil, lima beans or grass seed, label tape or marker, paper bag, watering can. Optional: Paper, pencil, penny, pebble, button

OBJECTIVE: Child will use the scientific method, giving the child experience predicting, testing, and drawing conclusions.

The child can perform an experiment to find out what the essentials of plant growth are—what a seed needs not just to sprout, but to grow into a healthy green plant. The child will be testing whether a seed can grow without light, without soil, without water, or must have all three. The child can start the experiment by filling three of the cups with soil and one with a crumpled newspaper. Plant a seed in each one. The child can then place the

cups on a windowsill and put a paper bag over one of the cups with soil. Help the child make labels using label tape or write on cups with a marker. Label the bean planted in newspaper, "no soil." Label the bean under a paper bag, "no sun." Label one of the remaining beans, "no water." Label the last one, "soil, sun, water." The child can now water each of the beans except the one designated no water. (Make sure the "no sun" plant gets covered up after watering!) The child can check the plants daily and continue to add water to three of the plants to keep them moist during the duration of the experiment (a couple weeks). Invite the child to predict and observe which seeds grow into plants. To increase

the challenge, the child can chart the results or draw his or her observations. To continue this activity, after the child has determined that it takes soil, water, and light for good green growth, the child can plant different items (a lima bean, a penny, a pebble, a button) and provide each with soil, water, and light. The child can predict which will grow.

41 TAKE STOCK OF A ROCK

There are so many ways to look at a rock!

WHAT YOU'LL NEED: Rocks, paper clips, yarn, scissors, balance scale, tub of water, magnifying glass. Optional: Paper, pencil

OBJECTIVE: Child will compare, sort, and classify.

Invite the child to collect rocks and then look—really look! The child can measure, compare, describe, and draw the rocks. The rocks can be measured by finger lengths, paper clips, or with pieces of yarn cut to the length of each rock. The weights of the rock can be compared using a balance scale and they can be ordered by weight. Their textures can be compared using fingers or even cheeks (gently!). They can be examined dry and wet, and examined more carefully both ways using a magnifying glass.

HOW BIG AROUND? 42

You are this tall, but how big around are you?

WHAT YOU'LL NEED: Yarn, scissors, apple, potato, radish, pumpkin, watermelon (or other fruits and vegetables on hand)

OBJECTIVE: Child will use measurement activities to encourage prediction and comparison, as well as developing experience and practice measuring.

It's common to measure how short, tall, long, or wide something is, but not how big around! Measuring the circumference of various fruits and vegetables can lead to surprising results when the round distances are spread out into flat lengths and compared to one another. The child can use yarn for measuring. Separate pieces of yarn can be precut to make the measuring easier. The child can measure around the fruit or vegetable with the yarn and cut the yarn to that size. He or she can then line up the strips and compare them.

A LITTLE PIECE OF EARTH

Look for seeds, seeds everywhere!

WHAT YOU'LL NEED: Spoon, plastic cup or jar, water, plastic sandwich bag, rubber band

OBJECTIVE: Child will predict and use observation skills.

Seeds are always present wherever there's dirt and soil. In winter many seeds lie dormant. In spring and summer, seeds wait until the conditions are just right and then begin to grow. The child can be a seed detective and find out just what seeds may be secretly lying around in the dirt! The child can scoop up dirt and place it in the jar or cup. The jar of soil can be brought indoors and moistened with a little bit of water. Help the child make a greenhouse by covering the cup with a plastic bag and a rubber band. Place the jar in a sunny window and check daily to see what seeds were hidden in the soil.

GOOD VIBRATIONS

Use only your breath to make fun sounds!

WHAT YOU'LL NEED: Cardboard tubes, variety of narrow-necked plastic bottles, straws, paper

OBJECTIVE: Child will make comparisons and draw conclusions.

Vibrations produce sounds. The child can make vibrations with columns of air and change the sounds by changing the columns. Encourage the child to experiment (noisily) by blowing into the different items and noticing the different kinds of sounds that can be achieved. Extend by challenging the child to make different sizes and shapes of tubes with paper and observe how the sounds change as the tube is changed.

45 FLOWER SCRUTINY

So many flowers—how are they alike and how are they different?

WHAT YOU'LL NEED: Four different kinds of flowers, scissors, plastic knife, magnifying glass. Optional: Paper, pencil, crayons

OBJECTIVE: Child will observe, compare, classify, and explore.

Flowers are a part of plants, and they come in all different sizes, shapes, colors, and smells! Invite the child to compare four different kinds of flowers and note all the similarities and differences. The child can use the magnifying glass to look closely. The scissors and knife can be used to dissect the flowers and look inside them. For a more advanced activity, have the child record the findings (or dictate them to you). The child can draw pictures of the different flowers, record their colors, or count how many petals each flower has. Additional flowers can be added to the study. (Flowers can be obtained from the garden or from a supermarket—yesterday's wilted bunch is often available at a discount!)

The most effective kind of education is that a child should play amongst lovely things.
Plato

FLOWING FOUNTAINS

Water play is engaging, but it can be artistic, too.

 WHAT YOU'LL NEED: Several empty plastic milk cartons or plastic bottles, large nail, measuring cups or water containers

OBJECTIVE: Child will observe, compare, and draw conclusions.

Have the child experiment with simple fountains. Make water fountains with the child by punching holes in several plastic containers and then filling them with water. (Be sure to do this either outside or in the house inside a plastic tub!) The holes can be punched in a row vertically, around the bottle at the same level, or randomly around the container. Encourage the child to come up with different plans for hole punching designs. The child can fill the containers and observe and describe how the water flow is different depending on where the holes are.

NATURE COLLECTION

Pinecones, seeds, leaves, and flowers—nature has so many treasures!

 WHAT YOU'LL NEED: Shopping bag, containers for sorting, clear contact paper

OBJECTIVE: Child will sort and classify.

Go on a walk together in the neighborhood or in a local park. Take along a shopping bag and invite the child to look for and collect interesting nature objects, such as twigs, leaves, feathers, pebbles, and rocks. When you return home, challenge the child to sort and describe the objects. The child can also make window pictures by laying items on top of a piece of clear contact paper, sticky side up. After objects have been arranged, place a second sheet of contact paper on top, sticky side down, to seal the items.

WEIGH AWAY

Light, lighter, lightest—which is which?

 WHAT YOU'LL NEED: Hanger, hole punch or large nail, two empty margarine tubs of equal size, yarn, assorted items (toy cars, blocks, rocks)

OBJECTIVE: Child will use predicting, testing, weighing, comparing, and ordering skills.

A simple balance scale can be made easily with help from the child, and then once completed can provide the child with the opportunity to independently make weight comparisons for a myriad of toys and household objects. To make the scale, punch or poke three holes equidistantly around the rim of the two margarine tubs. The child can help make the holes. Cut six pieces of yarn all the same size and thread one end of a piece of yarn though a hole and tie it to the tub. Repeat for all holes and all pieces of yarn. Then tie the three strings of one tub on one end of a hanger and the three strings from the other tub on the other end. Now you have a balance scale! The scale can be hung on a doorknob. Once the scale is set up, encourage the child to gather together an assortment of items and test predictions about which things will be heavier or lighter than others. To make the activity more challenging, the child can continue to compare a group of objects until able to order them all from lightest to heaviest. The child can also make predictions about how many of a lighter object it will take to equal the weight of a heavier one.

SCAVENGER HUNT

49

What's all around? Let's find out!

 WHAT YOU'LL NEED: Check off list, clipboard or cardboard and large paper clip, pencil, old magazines, nontoxic white glue, yarn

OBJECTIVE: Child will refine observation skills, and emergent reading is encouraged.

Children are naturally observant of their surroundings, so go on a scavenger hunt and make a game out of it. Create a list of things to look for. The list can be pictorial, either line drawings or pictures cut from magazines and glued to the list, or words for young readers. Items pictured might include a dog, bird, mailbox, stop sign, something orange, something yellow. Invite the child to carry the list as you take a walk through the neighborhood, the child checking off each item discovered (tie the pencil to the clipboard with yarn).

50

SHAKIN' UP THE CREAM!

Butter is easy to make with a little muscle power.

 WHAT YOU'LL NEED: Small clear jar, ½ pint heavy cream, cup, plastic knife, plate, crackers

OBJECTIVE: Child will observe and participate in the process of change.

Cracker snacks spread with homemade butter are delicious! Have everyone wash hands, then let the child pour the cream into the jar and tighten the lid. (Adult should make sure lid is on tightly.) Take turns shaking the jar. Encourage the child to use muscles and shake hard. After ten minutes, the cream will be turning to butter and the whey separating. Let the child observe the results during the process. The child can pour the whey into a cup and taste it if curious. The butter left in the jar will be soft and easy to spread. For more challenge, invite the child to compare the taste, texture, and color to store-bought unsalted butter and describe what is the same and what is different.

44

IT'S ALL IN MY HEAD—
IMAGINING & PRETENDING!

Imagination is the doorway to creativity, but it is the window to learning as well! Children use their imaginations to help them integrate all that they see and hear around them. They explore relationships through play-acting and learn to empathize with others through dramatic play. They share their ideas, problem solve, and develop thinking skills through storytelling. They learn to plan and visualize as they construct buildings and paint pictures. And in all these activities, children experience the joy of self-expression. Imagining and pretending are powerful tools for discovery. They are tools that help children make sense of the world and also help express what they feel and who they are.

51 WEB WEAVING

Web weaving is made easy with a little paint squeezing!

 WHAT YOU'LL NEED: Paper, crayons or markers, paint or nontoxic colored glue in squeeze bottles

OBJECTIVE: Child will use creative thinking to express ideas through artistry.

Provide the child with a paper that has a large dot (approximately ½ inch in diameter) drawn anywhere on the paper. The dot is the start of a spider who needs a web! Encourage the child to draw legs for the spider. The child can then create the spider's web by squeezing paint or colored glue in any kind of line design. To make the activity richer, read a story about a spider, fiction or nonfiction, before asking the child to weave a web for his or her imaginary spider.

HAT PARADE

52

*A hodgepodge of hats opens the door
to delightful drama!*

WHAT YOU'LL NEED: Paper plates, hole punch, yarn, nontoxic white glue, ribbon, tissue paper, construction paper, scissors, stapler, markers, newspaper, masking tape

OBJECTIVE: Child will use creative thinking and dramatic play.

The child can make an assortment of hats, with adult help, and then use them for dramatic play and story invention.

Paper Plate Hat: Thread and tie two pieces of thick yarn through holes punched on either side of a paper plate. The child can decorate the top of the hat by gluing on ribbons, tissue paper, and strips of construction paper. When completed, the yarn strips can be tied to hold the hat on the child's head. For a variation, a large hole can be cut in the middle of the paper plate so that the hat is a brim only.

Band and Strip Hat: Use a thick strip of construction paper to make a band that fits around the child's head. The ends of the band are stapled together. The child can use additional strips of construction paper to make the crown of the hat by stapling them in arches from one side of the band to the other, making one or many arches. The child can glue on decorations or use markers to color on the strips and arches.

Cylinder Hat: A large piece of construction paper is made into a cylinder to fit on the child's head. The child can cut slits all around the bottom edge (approximately 1½ inches long), and then bend the cut paper out. Cut a hole in the middle of a paper plate the size of the cylinder, then let the child slide the plate over the top of the cylinder to where the slits begin. The child can glue the slits to the bottom of the plate to create a brim. The child can then decorate the hat.

Brimmed Newspaper Hat: Open several sheets of newspaper. The newspaper is placed over the child's head. A piece of masking tape is taped around the crown of the child's head to fit, and then the child can trim the brim. Decorate!

MAGNETIC MELODRAMA

Use magnets to keep paper actors on the move!

 WHAT YOU'LL NEED: Tagboard, blocks or books, index cards, crayons or markers, nontoxic white glue, paper clips, magnets

OBJECTIVE: Child will develop expressive-language skills.

The child can create a stage for paper actors by setting a piece of tagboard across two stacks of blocks or books. The actors are made by folding back the bottom third of an index card and drawing a picture of a person, an animal, or an imaginary creature on the top portion. A paper clip is then glued to the bottom of the folded back portion. When the glue is dry, the child can place all the actors on the stage and make up stories about them. While doing the storytelling, the child can move the characters around from underneath the stage by using the magnet. For a melodramatic magnet variation, the child can make refrigerator magnet faces! Purchase round magnets (approximately 1 inch across) at a hardware or hobby store. Cut circles the same size out of stiff paper. The child can draw faces on the stiff paper with markers and glue the paper to the magnets.

That living word awakened my soul, gave it light, joy, set it free!
Helen Keller

CASTOFF CREATIONS

54

Create alluring art from old castoffs and clutter!

WHAT YOU'LL NEED: Cardboard, nontoxic white glue, cardboard tubes, paper scraps, old hardware pieces, buttons, yarn, ribbon, straws, general household junk

OBJECTIVE: Child will express ideas through artistry.

Gather an assortment of paper scraps and old household odds and ends. Provide the child with cardboard for a base and nontoxic white glue for constructing. The child can make selections from the collection and assemble and glue assorted items together to create personal sculptures. To simplify the activity, provide the child with five to eight cast-off items, and challenge him or her to make a creation using all the items. (If the child is under three, be sure to keep items large enough to avoid a choking hazard.)

55

WHAT KIND OF CREATURE ARE YOU?

Imaginary creatures come to life while molding with modeling clay!

WHAT YOU'LL NEED: Plasticine, aluminum foil or plastic mat, toothpicks, buttons, yarn, ribbon, pebbles

OBJECTIVE: Child will use creative thinking and imagination.

The child can use plasticine to create and invent creatures. Cover the work surface with aluminum foil or a plastic mat. The child can model and shape the clay into a creature and then use accessories to make impressions in the clay or for animal parts. Encourage the child to describe the animal. To make the activity more challenging, invite the child to talk about how the animal moves, what it likes to eat, where it lives, and other zoological details of its pretend existence.

SUIT UP FOR OUTER SPACE!

Turn paper bags into space suits and take off!

WHAT YOU'LL NEED: Large brown paper bags, scissors, masking tape, markers.
Optional: Thick yarn

OBJECTIVE: Child will use creative thinking.

The child can create space shoes by putting a large paper bag over each shoe and crumpling up the ends to make them snug on the ankles. Tape the shoes at the ankles with masking tape. For space sleeves, cut the bottoms out of two large bags. Crumple the bags and tape at the wrists and upper arms. For a helmet, cut a large window out of a bag and place it over the child's head. The child can decorate the space suit before it is donned. To make the suit reusable, use a thick piece of yarn rather than masking tape. To extend the space play, provide space snacks for the child: Pour juice or spoon pudding into a plastic bag, insert a straw, and seal snugly with a twist tie.

FAVORITE STORY CASSETTE

57

Listen to a favorite story again, and again, and again, and again!

WHAT YOU'LL NEED: Tape player, cassette, favorite book, bell

OBJECTIVE: Child will use listening skills.

Make a cassette recording of one of the child's favorite stories. The child can listen as you read the story. Signal the child whenever it is time to turn a page. The child can then ring a bell. This will be the signal for the child to turn a page when looking at the book and listening to the tape independently.

CARDBOARD CRITTERS

58

Construct creatures from a conglomeration of cardboard boxes.

 WHAT YOU'LL NEED: Empty cereal and food boxes, cardboard tubes, construction paper, scissors, nontoxic white glue, paint

OBJECTIVE: Child will use problem-solving and creative-thinking skills.

The child can choose just the right boxes and cardboard tubes and can glue them together to turn them into animals. The animals can be painted, and construction paper can be glued on to create ears and tails. To make the activity simpler, reduce the variables! Provide the child with two differently sized boxes and a few cardboard tubes to create a unique animal.

59 # SNACK FACE AT MY PLACE

Smile at a snack that will smile back!

WHAT YOU'LL NEED: Plate, plastic knife, rice cakes, peanut butter or cream cheese, toppings (olives, carrot slices, pineapple slices, apple slices, raisins, walnut halves)

OBJECTIVE: Child will use creative thinking.

The child can create snack faces on rice cakes (or any round cracker or bread). Have everyone wash their hands before beginning. Invite the child to spread peanut butter or cream cheese on a rice cake. Mouths, noses, and eyes (and ears and eyebrows and mustaches, if desired!) are created by placing assorted toppings on the spread. The child can tell about the face snack and then eat it as a treat. To make the activity more unusual and intriguing, invite the child to create three or four different faces. Then carefully cut each of the faces in half. The child can mix and match the faces before eating them!

MASK MAKING

60

*Take part in mask making, then masquerade
while play acting!*

 WHAT YOU'LL NEED: Large paper bags, scissors, crayons, nontoxic white glue, ribbon, yarn, construction paper, fabric scraps. Optional: Paper plate, cardboard

OBJECTIVE: Child will use creative thinking to explore dramatic play.

Turn large paper bags into masks! Place a bag over the child's head and carefully mark the eye holes. Remove the bag and cut the holes or invite the child to cut them. Recheck the eye holes for good visibility, and adjust holes for best viewing. The child can then decorate the bag by coloring it or gluing on paper pieces, fabric scraps, yarn, and ribbon. Ribbon and yarn can be glued on the top of the bag to create hair. Fabric scraps or paper can be used to create animal ears. For a simpler mask, cut eye holes in a paper plate and decorate it. Glue a strip of cardboard to the bottom of the plate to use as a handle to hold the mask.

BUILDING WITH BOXES

61

A box is not just a box, a box can be anything at all!

 WHAT YOU'LL NEED: Variety of large and small cardboard boxes, paper plates, cardboard tubes, buttons, spools, string, plastic bottle tops, nontoxic white glue, markers. Optional: Paint, brush, water container

OBJECTIVE: Child will use problem-solving and creative-thinking skills.

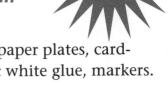

Provide an assortment of boxes in various sizes and then challenge the child to invent ways to use them. The boxes might become a vehicle for riding in, a computer, the control panel of a spaceship, a stove, etc. The child can glue boxes together or glue accessories to the boxes. The boxes can also be painted or decorated with markers.

MAY I SERVE YOU?

62

Properly prepared, playdough can become a delectable dreamed-up dinner!

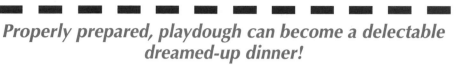

WHAT YOU'LL NEED: Playdough, paper plates, cooking utensils (rolling pin, cookie cutters, garlic press, plastic tableware). Optional: Old magazines, scissors, nontoxic white glue

OBJECTIVE: Child will use creative-thinking and expressive-language skills.

The child can use simple utensils to create pretend foods out of the playdough. The meals can be served on paper plates on a table surrounded by stuffed animals or willing adults—or both! The child can plan a whole menu for the meal or stick to one specialty dish. For more food preparation play, the child can turn the pretend kitchen into a restaurant with menus for the guests.

63 GOGGLES FOR GIGGLES!

Goggles lead to silly parts to play!

WHAT YOU'LL NEED: Egg carton, scissors, yarn, stapler, markers

OBJECTIVE: Child will explore different stories and roles as well as creative expression.

Create goggles and half masks using a portion of an egg carton. Two egg cups are cut out together from the egg carton—be sure to include the portion bordering either side. Measure and staple a length of yarn to each outer side so the goggles can be slipped on and off. Cut holes in the bottom of each cup so the child can look through the goggles. The child can decorate the goggles and use them for dramatic play. For variety, one egg cup can be used to make a mask that just goes over the nose (be sure to cut some air holes).

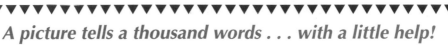

PICTURE TALK

A picture tells a thousand words . . . with a little help!

WHAT YOU'LL NEED: Colored chalk, paper, water, bowl, tablespoon, sugar. Optional: Light-colored tempera paint, dark-colored construction paper

OBJECTIVE: Child will use observation and language skills to interpret and express ideas.

The child can draw a story and then talk about it to share it! For brightly colored picture stories, soak colored chalk in sugared water. The child can measure several tablespoons of sugar into a bowl of water, stir it, and add the chalk to the bowl. Soak the chalk ten minutes. The child can then create a colorful picture story and tell about it. For another way to explore picture and story drawing using chalk, pour a little white or light-colored tempera paint into a small container. The child can dip the colored chalk (not presoaked) into the paint before drawing with it on dark-colored construction paper. The lines will be the same color as the chalk but will be edged with the light-colored tempera paint.

WHAT WOULD YOU DO?

Share the solution with a display of dramatic action!

OBJECTIVE: Child will use problem-solving skills.

Take turns making up imaginary situations and challenge one another to act out what one might do. For example, "What would you do if five lions walked in the kitchen while you were eating lunch?" "What would you do if you woke up in the morning and you discovered you'd been sleeping in a tree?" "What would you do if the cat came to the kitchen table and asked for breakfast cereal?"

66 WHAT'S DOT?

Start with one dot and go from there!

WHAT YOU'LL NEED: Paper, crayons, stick-on dots, scissors

OBJECTIVE: Child will use problem-solving and creative-thinking skills.

Place one stick-on dot anywhere on a paper. The child can decide what the dot will become and draw the rest of the picture around the dot. (The dot could be an animal head, the tip of someone's hat, a ball children are throwing, etc.) If the child enjoys this activity, on another day provide a paper with a small hole in it as a picture challenge. Cut out a hole approximately 1 inch in diameter anywhere on the paper, or have the child tell you how big to cut the hole and where. Invite the child to draw a picture around the hole, incorporating the hole into the picture any way he or she would like. (It might be a hole a worker is digging, the open mouth of a bear, the moon, or part of a design.)

ABSTRACT ART 67

Name that painting!

WHAT YOU'LL NEED: Art book with pictures of abstract art (available at library), paper, paint, water container, sponges

OBJECTIVE: Child will use creative-thinking, interpretive, and language skills.

Look at pictures of abstract modern art paintings together and talk about how the artist might have created them. Share and talk about the titles of the paintings. Encourage the child to share ideas about how the artists might have come up with the painting names. Then invite the child to make modern art paintings of his or her own by splattering, folding the paper in half, or using sponges to paint blobs and shapes.

ALL ABOARD

Turn boxes into buses and tour the town!

WHAT YOU'LL NEED: Chairs or boxes, stuffed animals, paper plate, paper, scissors, markers, tape

OBJECTIVE: Child will use dramatic play to explore transportation.

The child can become a bus driver, train conductor, or an airplane pilot by using a few simple props. Trains, planes, or buses can all be easily imagined and created using large cardboard boxes alone or along with chairs. If the child is using boxes, they can be decorated to look like a taxi, car, plane, train, etc. A paper plate can be a steering wheel. Stuffed animals become passengers. Tickets and signs can be made with paper and markers. The child can then transport people and animals around the city, state, and nation! If the child shows continued interest in vehicle play, check out some library books on transportation. The child can look at the pictures to learn more about different vehicles and to get fresh ideas for dramatic play!

To know is nothing at all; to imagine is everything.
Anatole France

IMAGINARY SNOW

69

Create clouds and snow with silky, fluffy, smooth, and puffy white foam!

WHAT YOU'LL NEED: Shaving cream (nonmenthol!), waterproof smock, plastic tablecloth, plastic animals, cars

OBJECTIVE: Child will explore tactile experiences while creating stories.

Spread a plastic tablecloth over a table and spray with mounds of shaving cream. Wearing a smock, the child can mold and mush and slosh the foamy cream, enjoying and talking about the texture. On a warm summer day, this activity can be done outside in a bathing suit! (Remind the child not to rub his or her eyes with foamy fingers.) The child can form the foam into puffy clouds, snowy mountains, imaginary white worlds, or have fun making patterns and designs in it. Plastic animals, cars, and other toys can be used for active story-making.

STORY CARDS

70

Use interesting pictures to elicit entertaining tales!

WHAT YOU'LL NEED: Magazines, scissors, paper, nontoxic white glue

OBJECTIVE: Child will use creative-thinking, sequencing, and problem-solving skills.

Encourage the child to choose assorted subjects, such as people, animals, places, foods, shoes, etc., from magazines. The child can then cut out 10 to 12 of the pictures. Glue each picture onto a separate piece of paper to create the story cards. When the glue is dry, turn the papers upside down and spread them out. The child chooses three of the story cards to turn over and then makes up a story that includes all three pictures. The story cards can also be used for cooperative storytelling. One person chooses a card from the upside down cards and begins a story about that picture. The next person chooses another card and makes up the next part of the story, incorporating that picture—then keep going!

TELEPHONE TALK

Consult, confer, and converse with pretend people!

WHAT YOU'LL NEED: Toy telephone, notepad, pencil, large cardboard box, child-size chair

OBJECTIVE: Child will use imaginative and language skills.

With the help of a toy phone and a pretend phone booth the child can improvise and act out imaginary conversations. The child can dramatize phone calls to real or pretend people or animals. The child might also want to call characters from favorite stories! A pencil and notepad can be used for taking messages. A large cardboard box can be turned into a telephone booth by standing it on its side and placing a child-size chair inside. To give this activity an added challenge, provide a "phone book" or cards with names or pictures and phone numbers for real or pretend people or animals. The child can read the numbers and dial them on the play phone.

The direction in which education starts a man will determine his future life.

Plato

72 WHAT THE SUNDAY FUNNIES REALLY SAY

▼▼▼▼▼▼▼▼▼▼▼▼▼▼▼▼▼▼▼▼▼▼▼▼▼▼▼

Make up new stories for old funnies!

 WHAT YOU'LL NEED: Sunday newspaper comics, white stick-on labels, pen

OBJECTIVE: Child will use interpretive and sequencing skills.

Place white stick-on labels inside the word bubbles of the Sunday funnies. The child can look at the sequence of pictures of a comic and make up a story to go along with the sequence. The child can dictate the words that each character says and the adult can write the words in the bubbles. Read the new story back to the child.

ACTING OUT MUSICAL STORIES 73

● ●

Listen and retell a story using music and action but no words!

 WHAT YOU'LL NEED: Music that tells a story with instruments (Prokofiev's *Peter and the Wolf*, Saint-Saëns's *The Carnival of the Animals*, or "The March of the Wooden Soldiers" from Tchaikovsky's *The Nutcracker Suite*). These are often available at libraries.

OBJECTIVE: Child will use creative-thinking and interpretive skills.

Share a piece of story-based instrumental music with the child. Talk briefly about the story before listening to the music. Then listen together, sharing reactions to the story portrayal. Listen a second time, inviting the child to act out the story to the music. For a variation, invite the child to listen to instrumental music that doesn't illustrate any specific story. Let the child invent his or her own story to be acted out in movement to the music.

BUILDING BIG BLOCKS FOR BIG BLOCK BUILDINGS

Build big tall towers with do-it-yourself grocery bag blocks!

 WHAT YOU'LL NEED: Big brown grocery bags, newspaper, masking tape

OBJECTIVE: Child will use creative-thinking, problem-solving, and visual-perception skills.

The child can make giant blocks by wadding up old newspapers and stuffing them into large brown grocery bags. Slip a filled bag into a second bag to seal off the open end. Secure the second bag with masking tape. The child can create a whole set of big blocks that can be towered high and will tumble safely! Children may soon grow tired of making blocks, so adults should make this a project that spans a number of days, or adults can make most of the blocks before the child sits down to make a few. Add diversity by creating an additional set of lunch-bag blocks.

WHIMSICAL WORDS

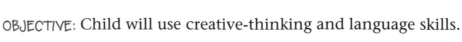

Compose poetic nonsense!

OBJECTIVE: Child will use creative-thinking and language skills.

Read the child poetry that uses made-up or nonsensical words. Explain that sometimes poets use pretend words to make a poem silly, fun, or different. Talk about the nonsense words you hear in the poems you read and why the poet might have used them. Then together create invented poetry using whimsical word sounds in place of real words. The poems can be all made-up word sounds or include just one or two nonsense words here and there for fun. For a challenge, have a pretend conversation using only made-up words!

HOW DOES AN ELEPHANT DANCE?

76

Just imagine some silly things—elephants dancing and walruses waltzing!

WHAT YOU'LL NEED: Music

OBJECTIVE: Child will use creative movement to express ideas.

The child can listen to a piece of music and imagine and act out how an elephant might move and dance to that piece of music. Ask the child to picture the elephant dancing! How would he move to the music? Would he take big steps or little ones? Light or heavy? Fast or slow? Then play music of another mood or tempo and invite the child to portray how the elephant might dance to that music! For a greater challenge, the child can imagine how other animals might move and dance to the same pieces of music.

77

BIRTHDAY FOR A BEAR

Everyone deserves a birthday party, even bears and other animals!

WHAT YOU'LL NEED: Stuffed animals, paper plates, party hats, playdough, crayons, paper, scissors, plastic knife, wrapping paper, ribbons

OBJECTIVE: The child will use creative thinking and dramatic play.

The child can plan a party for a stuffed bear or another favorite stuffed toy. The child can make decorations, decide on games, create a playdough birthday cake, and even make and wrap a gift to give to the birthday animal. The child can also make party invitations to "send" to other stuffed toys and animals. Then it's time to have fun, play the games, sing "Happy Birthday," unwrap presents, and enjoy the cake!

PROLIFIC PUPPETRY

Gloves, mittens, and old clean socks turn into puppets for friendly talks!

WHAT YOU'LL NEED: Clean old gloves, clean old socks, scissors, nontoxic white glue, felt scraps, paper scraps, yarn. Optional: Old mittens

OBJECTIVE: Child will use creative thinking and expressive language.

Glove Puppets: The child can glue felt or paper scraps onto each finger of an old glove to turn them into five friendly fellows. Glue yarn to the tip of each finger for hair. The child can then wear the glove and create conversations among the five friends.

Finger Puppets: Cut the fingers off an old glove. The child can create a face for each finger (or one finger) the same as was done for the glove puppets. These finger puppets can be used individually. (The five fellows don't always have to stick together anymore!)

Sock Puppets: The child can create a face on a clean old sock by gluing on felt, paper scraps, and yarn. The child can then slip the whole sock on over a hand and use it as a hand puppet to talk and tell stories. (Mittens can also be used!)

I hear and forget.
I see and remember.
I do and understand.

Chinese proverb

79 CORK CREATIONS

Create critters and other things with cork!

WHAT YOU'LL NEED: Corks, pipe cleaners, construction paper, scissors, nontoxic white glue, yarn, markers

OBJECTIVE: Child will use creative-thinking skills.

The child can construct people, animals, and other things and inventions by gluing corks together. Pipe cleaners can be used and inserted into the cork for arms, legs, or machine parts. Paper scraps can be glued on to make clothing, hats, animal ears, or decorations. Yarn can also be glued on for decoration, for hair, or to make a tail. The child can use markers to make eyes, ears, or noses where needed! To simplify, individual corks can be made into little cork people and used for play. Cut strips of colored paper that are half as wide as the corks. The child can glue the colored paper strips around the bottom of the cork for clothing. The child can then draw eyes, nose, mouth, and hair on the cork with markers.

ITTY BITTY TEENY TINY ME 80

Pretend to be teeny tiny for a little itty bit of fun!

OBJECTIVE: Child will use creative-thinking and problem-solving skills.

Child can make believe he or she is very, very small and do everything in an itty bitty teeny tiny way: Take itty bitty teeny tiny steps when walking. Use an itty bitty teeny tiny voice when talking. Take itty bitty teeny tiny bites of food when eating. Make an itty bitty teeny tiny drawing on a teeny tiny itty bitty piece of paper. Encourage the child to think of many different actions and activities to try out in a small way. Later on, the child can try doing everything in a GREAT BIG GIANT WAY.

STEPPING INTO A STORY

Act in character for a dramatic day!

81

 OBJECTIVE: Child will use creative-thinking, problem-solving, and interpretive skills.

After reading a favorite story, invite the child to be the character in the story as you go about your daily routine. Encourage the child to imagine how the story character might eat lunch, clean up toys, pet the dog, etc. What might the story character say when the phone rings? How would the character wash his face? Challenge the child to act in character while going about some of the normal activities of the day. For a variation, instead of dramatizing one character doing different things, take turns performing the same action as various characters from different stories.

82

WHAT KIND OF CAT IS THAT?

Fashion a family of felines from precut paper parts.

 WHAT YOU'LL NEED: Large index cards folded and cut as shown, markers or crayons

OBJECTIVE: Child will use creative-thinking and language skills.

Provide the child with precut cat bodies, heads, and tails as shown. The cat body should be cut from an index card folded in half so that the cat can stand upright. Cut a slit at the front end and back end of the top of the cat body for the head and tail. The child can decorate the cat's body, tail, and head. Then the child puts a cat together by slipping a head and tail into slits at the front and back of the body. The child can make one, two, three, or more cats depending on interest. Invite the child to describe and tell about the finished cats.

slits

fold + cut

83

MY MAGIC SEED

Plant an imaginary picture seed and water it with words!

WHAT YOU'LL NEED: Story about magical seeds or magic object, paper, lima bean, nontoxic white glue, crayons

OBJECTIVE: Child will use creative-thinking and expressive-language skills.

Read a story together that is about a magic seed or about any kind of seed planting (*Jack and the Beanstalk* is a good choice). Then give the child a paper that has a lima bean glued at the bottom. Tell the child that the bean on the paper is a magic seed that can grow into anything. Explain that the way the seed grows is by drawing. Invite the child to draw a picture that shows what the seed grows into and to tell a story about it. For a simpler variation, after reading a story about seed growth, invite the child to curl up into a small seed and dramatize the seed's growth into a plant. Add music to further inspire plant growth!

One clear idea is too precious a treasure to lose.
Caroline Gilman

TUBE ART

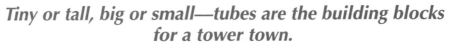

Tiny or tall, big or small—tubes are the building blocks for a tower town.

WHAT YOU'LL NEED: Cardboard, cardboard tubes, scissors, nontoxic white glue, paint, brush, water container. Optional: Construction paper, tape

OBJECTIVE: Child will use creative-thinking and problem-solving skills.

Provide the child with a piece of cardboard to use as a base and an assortment of long and short cardboard tubes. (The adult can cut the tubes into different sizes to increase the variation.) The child can create a tower town by arranging and gluing the tubes onto the cardboard base. When the glue has dried and the towers are secure, the town can be painted. To increase the challenge, the child can make additional tubes with greater variation using construction paper. Help the child cut the paper into different lengths and then roll them into fat and skinny cylinders. Use tape to secure the tubes.

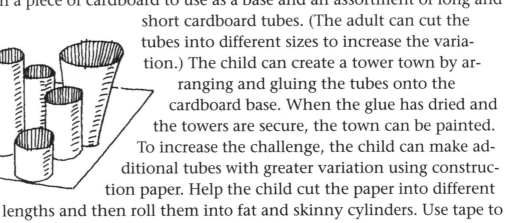

The brain is like a muscle. When it is in use we feel very good. Understanding is joyous.

Carl Sagan

85

PEEKABOO PLAYHOUSE

Puppets and other people have fun peeking in and out!

WHAT YOU'LL NEED: Construction paper, old magazines, scissors, nontoxic white glue, craft sticks, crayons

OBJECTIVE: Child will use creative-thinking and language skills.

Create a peekaboo playhouse using two different colored sheets of construction paper. Cut a door in one sheet of paper, cutting it on three sides so the flap can be opened and closed. Glue the two papers together just along the sides and the top. Puppet creatures are made by gluing pictures of people and animals cut out of magazines onto the end of craft sticks. The child could also draw the pictures instead of cutting them out of magazines. The child can then use the puppets by slipping them through the bottom opening between the two sheets of the playhouse so the puppets pop in and out of the door. You can also help the child make a larger playhouse with a door and some windows so the puppet has more choices to pop out of!

POEM PICTURES

86

Capture with colors the pictures that poems paint with words!

WHAT YOU'LL NEED: Paper, crayons. Optional: Finger paints, watercolor paints

OBJECTIVE: Child will use listening and interpretive skills.

Share a favorite poem with the child. Invite the child to describe what and who the poem is about and the scene where it might take place. The child can then draw a picture to illustrate the poem as imagined. For a variation, the child can create different illustrations for the poem (or other poems!) using different media, such as finger paints or watercolors.

MAGIC WAND

Make a magic wand and make magic!

 WHAT YOU'LL NEED: Newspaper, masking tape, markers, scissors

OBJECTIVE: Child will use creative-thinking and expressive-language skills.

Transform a piece of newspaper into a magic wand. Help the child roll the paper up into a skinny tube and secure it with masking tape. The child can decorate the wand with markers. Help the child cut fringe all around the top and tape the top of the strips together to create a bauble at the end. The child can then use the wand and invent magical consequences when the wand is waved or when someone is tapped by the wand. For a more brilliantly colored magic wand, use the Sunday funnies and colored masking tape.

MY PRIVATE PLACE

An old sheet is all that's needed to create a personal private suite!

 WHAT YOU'LL NEED: Sheet, paper, crayons, stuffed animals, books, trucks. Optional: Sheet, rope

OBJECTIVE: Child will use creative-thinking skills.

Drape a sheet over a table in order to make a tent area underneath. The cozy corner can

become a cave, barn, garage, or just a cozy corner. The child can supply the cozy corner with stuffed animals, books, paper, crayons, trucks, and other materials to use and play with in that private space. A private spot outdoors can also be created for a shady place to get away on a sunny day. Drape the sheet over a backyard table or over a rope tied between two trees.

CAPTURE THE WIND

89

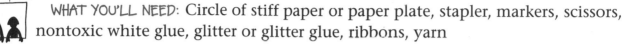

Make a wind catcher and invite the wind to come and play!

WHAT YOU'LL NEED: Circle of stiff paper or paper plate, stapler, markers, scissors, nontoxic white glue, glitter or glitter glue, ribbons, yarn

OBJECTIVE: Child will use creative-thinking and observation skills.

Invite the child to decorate a circle of stiff paper using markers and jazz it up with glitter and glue or glitter glue. (Adults: Glitter glue should not be used by children under three. If using glitter, be watchful—glitter can be dangerous if it gets in children's eyes!) When the decoration is complete, the child can then glue ribbon strips to the bottom of the circle so they hang down. Cut three pieces of yarn to the same length. Make three holes in the circle and thread a piece of yarn through each hole. Tie a knot in the yarn underneath the bottom of the circle. Tie the tops of the three strands of yarn together. Hang the wind catcher outside to catch the wind. To simplify, the child can use masking tape and several paper party streamers (about 3 feet long). Have the child observe how the strips dance with the wind.

> Beauty in things exists in the mind which contmplates them.
> David Hume

PAPER WARDROBE

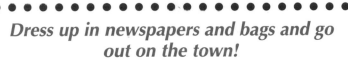

Dress up in newspapers and bags and go out on the town!

WHAT YOU'LL NEED: Large brown paper bags, newspaper, tape, scissors, stapler, large paper clips, markers

OBJECTIVE: Child will use creative thinking and dramatic play.

Large brown bags and newspaper can be cut and folded to create skirts, shirts, and vests to inspire dramatic play. The child can decorate the paper clothing with markers or wear the wardrobe as is.

Paper Bag Hula Skirt: Cut open a large brown paper bag and cut the bottom off. Fold one long edge down approximately 1 inch to make a waistband. At the other long side, cut slits in the skirt, stopping several inches short of the waistband. Secure the skirt on the child's waist with a paper clip.

Paper Bag Vest: Cut open a large brown paper bag and cut the bottom off. Cut armholes in the appropriate places and a V-neck. The child can fringe the bottom for a fancy vest.

Newspaper Poncho: Cut a vertical and horizontal slit in the middle of a large sheet of newspaper (approximately 10 inches long). The slits will allow the child to slip the paper overhead. Tape the end of each slit with masking tape to prevent tearing.

Newspaper Hula Skirt: Fold a sheet of newspaper four times to make a 2-inch waistband. For the skirt, tape together two sheets of newspaper. Cut slits from one long side, stopping several inches from the other side. Fold down the uncut end 1 inch to make it stronger. Take the skirt and insert the folded end into the fold of the waistband. Staple along the length. Fasten the skirt on the side with a large paper clip.

FOAM BOATS

Turn common foam into a starter kit for a neat, sleek sailing fleet!

WHAT YOU'LL NEED: Foam trays (from fruits or vegetables, washed well), chunks of foam cut from packing boxes, foam peanuts, corks, thread spools, toothpicks, bottle caps, twigs, cloth scraps, nontoxic white glue, plasticine clay. Optional: Egg cartons, milk containers, plastic containers, plastic lids, wood scraps

OBJECTIVE: Child will use problem-solving and creative-thinking skills.

The child can create one boat or assemble an entire navy. Foam trays washed with soap and water or chunks of packing foam can be used as the base for a ship or boat. The child can glue assorted accessories onboard the boat. A piece of fabric glued to a twig or toothpick can be inserted into the foam, glued on, or secured with plasticine. The child can float the boat (or boats) in a plastic tub, or they can accompany the child in the bathtub. If the child is especially fascinated by floating boats, provide a greater assortment of materials for boat bases for the child to explore. The child can also experiment with egg cartons, milk containers (empty and washed!), plastic containers, lids, or small wood pieces.

The doer alone learneth.
Freidrich Nietzsche

92 ONSTAGE

Stand onstage and show your stuff!

WHAT YOU'LL NEED: Wood blocks, duct tape, chairs, stuffed animals. Optional: Cardboard tube, paint, yarn, nontoxic white glue, tension rod, curtain

OBJECTIVE: Child will explore self-expression.

Create a stage by taping wooden blocks together with duct tape. The child can arrange chairs around the stage for the audience, which can include (or be made entirely of) stuffed animals and toys. The child can act, recite, tell stories, or sing on the stage. The child can make a microphone for the performances by gluing a long strip of yarn to a cardboard tube and painting the tube. To make a stage curtain, set the stage behind an open doorway and use a tension rod to hang a curtain in the doorway.

MUSIC LOOKS LIKE THIS 93

Happy, sad, fast, or slow? Listen to music, take your brush, and go!

WHAT YOU'LL NEED: Tape player, several cassettes, paper, paint, brushes

OBJECTIVE: Child will use listening and interpretive skills.

Gather together several musical selections that express different moods or tempos. Play one of the pieces. Ask the child how the music makes him or her feel. Encourage the child to share feelings in words or with movement. Then invite the child to paint to the music, painting the way the music makes the child feel. Afterward, or at another time, play a different selection and paint again.

94 LOTS OF PUPPETS AND MUPPETS!

Puppets and muppets parade some more . . . puppets to make by the score!

 WHAT YOU'LL NEED: **Lunch Bag Puppets:** Lunch-size paper bag, newspaper, markers, paper towel tube, yarn. Optional: Nontoxic white glue. **Spoon Puppets:** Old wooden spoons, markers. **Stick Puppets:** Old magazines, paper, markers, stiff paper, cardboard, scissors, nontoxic white glue

OBJECTIVE: Child will use creative thinking and expressive language.

Lunch Bag Puppets: The child can draw a face on a paper bag with markers. When the face is finished, the child can stuff the bag with crumpled newspaper. Insert a paper towel tube in the bottom of the bag and scrunch the end of the bag around the tube. Secure the tube to the bag by tying a piece of yarn around it. The tube then becomes the handle by which the child holds the puppet. (The child might also want to glue yarn on top of the bag for hair.)

Spoon Puppets: Gather together several old wooden spoons. The child can turn these into stick puppets by drawing faces on the backs of the spoons with markers.

Stick Puppets: The child can cut out pictures of people or animals from a magazine or make their own pictures and cut them out. Glue the cut-out pictures to stiff paper. The child then glues these people and animals to a strip of cardboard, which is used as a handle.

WALKING WAYS

Traipse and tramp to tell a tale!

OBJECTIVE: Child will use interpretive skills and body movement to communicate ideas.

Invite the child to act out walking in a variety of manners to communicate different ideas. Together with the child, think up a variety of situations and take turns acting out "walking as if." Here are some examples to start with:

Walk as if it's pouring rain.

Walk as if you're in a great hurry.

Walk as if you can't wait to get to the park.

Walk as if you don't want to go somewhere.

Walk as if you are being followed by a bear.

Walk as if you're on the moon.

To make the activity simpler, invite the child to walk across the room the way a cat, dog, mouse, duck, or elephant might.

> Everything should be made as simple as possible, but not simpler.
> Albert Einstein

96 — ORCHESTRA IN ONE

One child, five instruments, lots of music!

WHAT YOU'LL NEED: Cardboard tubes, empty oatmeal box, dry beans, wax paper, rubber band, paper plate, hole punch, pipe cleaners, bells, yarn, stapler, paint, brush. Optional: Elastic, stickers

OBJECTIVE: Child will use creative-thinking, listening, and problem-solving skills.

The child can make five simple instruments, explore each of them, and then, for a real challenge, try playing all five at one time!

Kazoo: The child can fit a piece of wax paper over the end of a toilet paper tube and secure it with a rubber band.

Maraca: The child can bend and staple closed one end of a toilet paper tube. The tube is then filled halfway with beans (or buttons or washers). Then bend the other end over and staple it closed. The child can paint the maraca. (Beware of choking hazard.)

Tambourine: Punch five or six holes around the edge of a paper plate. The child can attach small bells with pipe cleaners that are threaded through the holes.

Foot Drum: An empty oatmeal container becomes a drum. Have the child glue on yarn or add stickers for drama!

Jangle Anklet: String bells on a piece of yarn or sew them to a strip of elastic. Tie the yarn onto the child's ankle or wrist, or sew the ends of the elastic strip together so the child can easily slip it on and off without help.

Orchestra in One: The child taps on the drum with one foot, wiggles the jangle anklet with the other foot, waves the tambourine in one hand, shakes the maraca in the other, and hums on the kazoo—all at the same time!

PAPIER-MÂCHÉ PULP PLAY

Make papier-mâché pulp and mold away!

 WHAT YOU'LL NEED: Bowl, water, electric beater, newspaper, wheat paste, wire rack, paint, brush

OBJECTIVE: Child will use creative thinking and self-expression.

To make the pulp, fill a large bowl halfway with water. Add newspaper torn into strips and soak them overnight. Beat the mix to a pulp, then squeeze out excess water. Add wheat paste a little at a time. Beat again until smooth. The child can help with tearing the newspaper, with squeezing the water out of the mash, and by adding the wheat paste. When the pulp resembles clay and is smooth, the child can mold with it. To speed up drying time, hollow out the middle of the piece by turning it over and scooping out some material from the bottom. Molded pieces can be placed on a wire rack to dry. Allow plenty of drying time, and turn the pieces occasionally to keep them from getting moldy. When the pieces have dried thoroughly, the child can paint them.

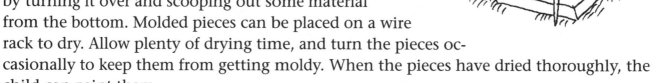

For all knowledge and wonder (which is the seed of knowledge) is an impression of pleasure in itself.
Francis Bacon

ENCHANTED POWER CAPE

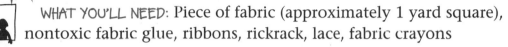

Make playtime magic with an enchanted power cape!

 WHAT YOU'LL NEED: Piece of fabric (approximately 1 yard square), nontoxic fabric glue, ribbons, rickrack, lace, fabric crayons

OBJECTIVE: Child will use dramatic play to explore different feelings and roles.

The child can make an enchanted power cape by decorating a large square of fabric. The child can color the square with fabric crayons or glue on pieces of lace, rickrack, and ribbon. When the child is finished, tie the two ends of the cape around the child's shoulders. This cape then transforms the child into a power being who can imagine and perform enchanted feats.

INVENT YOUR OWN MACHINE

Explore what makes machines work and invent a new one!

 WHAT YOU'LL NEED: Cardboard tubes, paper plates, small boxes, pipe cleaners, aluminum foil, junk from the hardware drawer, nontoxic white glue. Optional: Books, catalogs, magazines

OBJECTIVE: Child will use problem-solving and expressive-language skills.

The child can examine some simple nonelectrical machines, such as a manual eggbeater, a can opener, or a tricycle, and make observations and comparisons. The child can also look at pictures of machines in books, catalogs, or magazines and talk about what the machines can do and how people use them. Encourage the child to imagine a new kind of machine and what it might do. Let him or her create a machine by using the assortment of supplies. The child can decide how it works, what it does, and what it is named.

SEE WHAT I CAN MAKE AND DO—CREATING & PLAYING!

Creativity, play, and problem-solving are all wrapped up together and unfold together as children explore materials, create objects, and play games. The serious business of creating and playing engages children in constant problem-solving. They become divergent thinkers as they discover and invent new ways to paint or dance or build. They develop fluent and flexible thinking as they learn to see the world in more than one way. They grow in confidence and self-esteem as they create and express what they see from their own unique and personal perspectives!

100 MIX & FIX & FIZZLE & DRIZZLE

Make painting more interesting by making the paint first!

WHAT YOU'LL NEED: Clear vinegar, baking soda, cornstarch, corn syrup, measuring cup, teaspoon, bowl, spoon, food coloring, jar lids, brush, paper

OBJECTIVE: Child will measure, experiment, and observe changes.

Make homemade watercolor paints by using clear vinegar, baking soda, cornstarch, and corn syrup. The child can help with the measuring and mixing, and, of course, with the painting! Mix ¼ cup of clear vinegar and ¼ cup of baking soda in the bowl. Wait for the fizzle to stop and then add ¼ cup of cornstarch and 2 teaspoons of corn syrup. Stir. Pour the brew into empty jar lids, add a few drops of food color to each, and stir. The paint can be used immediately, or the child can wait until the paint dries to paint with them, adding a little water to the brush.

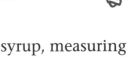

PRETTY PRINTED PATTERNS

*Create colorful patterns and designs
with sponge shapes.*

 WHAT YOU'LL NEED: Sponges, scissors, adding machine tape, tempera paint, plastic trays, water bowl. Optional: Paper towels

OBJECTIVE: Child will explore shapes and patterns.

Cut sponges into simple shapes, such as circles, squares, triangles, or stars, for sponge painting. Unroll a strip of adding machine tape. Pour two or three colors of paint into shallow trays. Dip a sponge into the water, then into the paint. The child can make random sponge painting decorations on the paper strip or can experiment and explore shape and color patterns. Several finished strips can be taped to the bottom of a wire hanger to make a simple decorative mobile. For a BIG variation of the

activity, cut shapes out of huge sponges and invite the child to make BIG sponge painting decorations and designs on a strip of white paper toweling.

TOP-NOTCH HOPSCOTCH

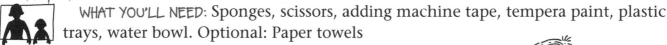

102

*Invent new twists (and hops) for
an old hopping standby.*

WHAT YOU'LL NEED: Chalk

OBJECTIVE: Child will use problem-solving and creative-thinking skills to plan and invent.

If child isn't familiar with hopscotch, teach it to the child and play a few games. Then invite the child to invent a new hopscotch game using chalk to draw lines and boxes on a sidewalk or patio. Encourage the child to think about how the new game will be played, including how to move (jump, hop, step), which way to go, and how to win the game!

LOOK, LISTEN, AND DO

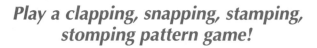

103

Play a clapping, snapping, stamping, stomping pattern game!

OBJECTIVE: Child will recognize, repeat, and create patterns.

Make up two-part patterns using clapping, patting, or other body movements. Demonstrate a pattern, such as clap-stomp-clap-stomp-clap-stomp, and then invite the child to repeat the pattern. As the child gains more experience, he or she can try a hand (or foot!) at making up two-part patterns to be repeated. Take turns making up patterns for one another to repeat and continue. Increase the challenge by including some three-part patterns in the game. For an even greater challenge, take turns adding an action to one another's pattern. For example, the adult might make up the pattern: clap-tap. The child can repeat it, and then change it by turning it into the three-part pattern: clap-tap-stomp. The adult can repeat it and then add one more: clap-tap-stomp-wiggle.

104

HOLEY LACIES

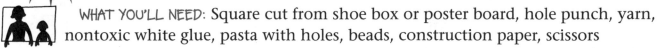

Make a lovely lacing by weaving in, out, around, over, and otherwise!

WHAT YOU'LL NEED: Square cut from shoe box or poster board, hole punch, yarn, nontoxic white glue, pasta with holes, beads, construction paper, scissors

OBJECTIVE: Child will use creative-thinking and small-muscle skills.

Provide the child with a stiff paper square that you have randomly punched holes in. The child can use a piece of yarn (stiffen the end with glue for easier lacing) to lace in and out of the holes. Tie a knot in the end of the yarn to keep it from pulling through. The lacing can occur as randomly as the holes! To enhance the design, add small pieces of construction paper with holes punched in them, pasta with holes, and beads to the mix! (Beware of choking hazard.)

BUBBLE PICTURES

105

Have double bubble fun indoors or outside in the sun!

WHAT YOU'LL NEED: Tempera paint, water, detergent, plastic bowl or pie tin, straw, straight pin, paper. Optional: Glycerin

OBJECTIVE: Child will experiment and observe cause and effect.

The child can use a straw to blow colorful painted bubbles and then create bubble pictures using the foam. This is a great outdoor summer project—it can get messy, but it's lots of fun! In a plastic bowl or pie tin, thin the tempera paint with water and add a healthy portion of liquid detergent to make it bubble easily. If you add a few drops of glycerin (available at a drugstore) the bubbles will be bigger. Have the child practice blowing out with a straw before blowing into the bubble solution to avoid any paint sipping. Use a pin to

prick a few holes around the top of the straw—this will also keep the child from sucking in the paint. Invite the child to blow into the soapy paint and experiment with bubble making. The child can make prints with the frothy foam by placing a piece of paper on top of the bubbles, gently pressing down, and then lifting the paper off.

I am still learning.
Michelangelo

106

PIZZA FOR ONE

Make a tasty personal pizza treat to eat!

 WHAT YOU'LL NEED: English muffins, grated cheese, tomato sauce, sliced vegetables (green peppers, olives, mushrooms, etc.), cutting board, paper plate, plastic knife, spoon, baking pan, pot holder, spatula. Optional: Magazines, scissors, nontoxic white glue

OBJECTIVE: Child will make choices and use descriptive language.

Start with washed hands! Together, cut and prepare the assorted toppings. The child can then create a personal pizza by spreading tomato sauce on half an English muffin, sprinkling it with grated cheese, and choosing toppings to put on top. Bake the private pizza in the oven for ten minutes at 350 degrees. Then eat! (Be sure sauce has cooled off!) The child can also make pizza pictures using a paper plate for the pizza and gluing on pictures of foods cut from magazines to make the toppings!

TAPE COLLAGE

107

Tape away—create a picture with nothing but tape!

WHAT YOU'LL NEED: Paper, scissors, several kinds of tape (clear tape, masking tape, colored masking tape, electrical tape, bandage tape)

OBJECTIVE: Child will explore and compare materials.

The child can experiment with a variety of different kinds of tapes. The tapes can be cut or torn and then stuck onto paper to make a tape collage. The child can compare the colors, textures, widths, as well as stickiness of the different tapes while using them to compose a picture. For a challenging variation, the child can use the tape to make a picture instead of a collage. The child can "draw" a house, tree, or face using tape to make all the lines and dots.

108 BEAUTIFUL BEADS

Mix, mold, and make beautiful beads!

WHAT YOU'LL NEED: ¾ cup flour, ½ cup salt, ½ cup cornstarch, water, bowl, unsharpened pencil or pipe cleaner, paint, brushes, yarn. Optional: Dowel

OBJECTIVE: Child will measure, follow steps in a process, and observe changes.

The child can help measure the dry ingredients into a bowl and then add the water to form a dough. Take turns kneading the dough. When the dough is pliable, the child can form beads by rolling round little handfuls of the dough into balls. The child can make holes in the beads with the end of a pencil or pipe cleaner. Set the beads out to dry. After they have dried, the child can paint them. When the paint is dry, the child can string the beads on yarn for wearing or for decoration! For a decoration variation, several strands of beads can be tied to a dowel with yarn for a pretty mobile.

SING A STORY

Make a story musical and sing it like a song.

OBJECTIVE: Child will use comprehension, sequencing, and language skills.

Ask the child to think of a favorite story or fairytale that he or she knows well and is fond of telling. Talk about the story together. Discuss who is in it and what the characters do. Then challenge the child to tell the story in song. Make up a tune, or use a familiar tune, and sing the start of the story as an example. Invite the child to continue the rest of the story in song, inventing the tune as he or she goes along.

DECORATING ME

Put a painting on a face!

WHAT YOU'LL NEED: Cornstarch, water, cold cream, food coloring, measuring spoons, paper cups, mirror, table covering, shower cap, smock, cotton swabs, facial tissue

OBJECTIVE: Child will use creative-thinking skills and dramatic play.

Make face paint together! Mix 1 teaspoon cornstarch, ½ teaspoon water, ½ teaspoon cold cream, and a drop of food coloring in a paper cup. Make several colors. Set a hand mirror on a table and cover the table with plastic or newspaper. The child can put on a shower cap and smock and sit at the table along with the adult. Let the child use the cotton swabs to paint his or her face while looking in the mirror. For more creative fun, challenge the child to sing a song, tell a story, or put on a little act when all painted up! (Caution the child about wiping the paint on clothing or other objects. Remove paint by using cold cream, soap, and water.)

WATCH A WATERWHEEL WORK

Construct a waterwheel that works, and watch the water turn it around!

WHAT YOU'LL NEED: Washed yogurt cup, scissors, plasticine clay, 2 toothpicks

OBJECTIVE: Child will experiment, predict, and observe.

Cut strips of plastic from the side of a yogurt cup. The child can create a waterwheel by placing the plastic strips in a row around a ball of plasticine clay. Place toothpicks on either side of the ball. The child then holds the waterwheel loosely by the toothpicks under a faucet of running water and watches the water make the ball spin around (toothpicks will turn as the waterwheel turns). The child can experiment further by changing the size and shape of the ball of clay, the distance between the paddles, the size of the paddles, how the water hits the paddles, etc.

LOOK! A BOOK!

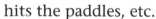

Add to a private library by making a personal book!

WHAT YOU'LL NEED: Construction paper, hole punch, pipe cleaners, markers

OBJECTIVE: Child will explore expressing ideas.

Cut construction paper into equal-sized squares. The child can count out five sheets of paper and punch a hole in the corner of each of the squares. Then the child can loop a pipe cleaner through the holes and twist the ends. The child can draw a story in the book and share it! Make blank books ahead of time for just the right moment—when the author is ready to write or draw! Another way to fasten the books is to punch several holes along one edge and weave a pipe cleaner through the holes.

FOOT PAINTING

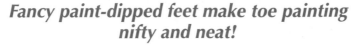

Fancy paint-dipped feet make toe painting nifty and neat!

WHAT YOU'LL NEED: Tempera paint, cornstarch, water, large shallow tray, newspaper, large paper, chair, pail of soapy water, towel, child-size chair or stool

OBJECTIVE: Child will explore self-expression through tactile (toeful!) experience.

The child can explore painting with feet and toes using finger paint placed in a large shallow tray or pan and a big sheet of paper on the ground. Make the homemade finger paint by mixing tempera with cornstarch and water. Spread plenty of newspapers on the floor first. Place a child-size chair or stool on the newspaper and a large sheet of paper in front of the chair. Put a shallow tray of finger paint (big enough for feet) next to it. (Have a pail of soapy water and a towel nearby!) The child can sit in the chair, dip feet into the paint, and then experiment painting with toes and feet.

For a variation, tape together several large pieces of paper to make a very large painting paper. Invite the child to paint standing up! The child can walk across the paper, drag feet, and make toe lines and other large paint strokes.

I do not teach children, I give them joy.
Isadora Duncan

DANCING WITH ELBOWS, NOSES, OR TOESIES

114

Dance and prance with different body parts!

WHAT YOU'LL NEED: Boombox, favorite CDs or tapes

OBJECTIVE: Child will use problem-solving to explore creative movement.

Play lively music on a cassette or CD and invite the child to dance to the music using just one body part! Allow child to stand or sit. How many ways can the child move to the music using only one body part? Two parts? Challenge the child to dance with just one toe, with a toe and an elbow, with just a nose, etc. For added challenge, make simple pictures of body parts on index cards and make the dance into a game. Have the child draw one or two cards to select which body parts to do a dance with. Or, each person chooses one card and uses the body part pictured to dance with a chosen body part of the other person!

115

WHIRLYBIRD

Make a paper 'copter and watch it whirl.

WHAT YOU'LL NEED: Paper, pencil, scissors

OBJECTIVE: Child will experiment and draw conclusions.

Using the diagram shown, help the child create a whirly-bird. After enlarging and copying the diagram onto paper, have the child help you cut on solid lines and fold on dotted lines. After folding in the sides of the bottom section, fold the tail section up. The child can then experiment dropping the whirlybird from high and low places and watching how it spins to the ground. The child can also make bigger and smaller whirlybirds to experiment with.

Wings

Fold out	Fold in

Fold to center | Fold to center

Fold UP

Tail

116 FOIL SCULPTURE

Transform junk into textured foil art!

WHAT YOU'LL NEED: Piece of cardboard, little items of household junk (screws, washers, paper clips, buttons), nontoxic white glue, water, brush, aluminum foil, soft cloth

OBJECTIVE: Child will use problem-solving to explore creative expression.

The child can start the sculpture by gluing assorted items with interesting shapes and sizes onto cardboard. (Be sure to supervise; small objects are choking hazards.) After the glue has dried and all the pieces are secured onto the cardboard, make a diluted glue solution. The child can paint the whole sculpture with the diluted glue. When the sculpture is covered with the diluted glue, have the child spread a sheet of foil over it, crunching it down to fit snuggly over all the shapes— then rubbing over the pieces with a finger to highlight the forms underneath. The child can then glue the edges of the foil over the cardboard with undiluted glue. Polish the sculpture with a soft cloth when fully dry! If the child enjoys working with the foil, another activity to experiment with is foil sculpture. The child can use the foil itself as the sculpting material. Sheets of foil can be crumpled and bent into different shapes, abstract or symbolic. The child can use tape to attach or hold the foil parts together.

MARSHMALLOW MINARET

Build towers and castles with easy to use (and eat!)
tools and materials.

WHAT YOU'LL NEED: Miniature marshmallows, colored toothpicks. Optional: Peanut butter, plastic knife

OBJECTIVE: Child will use creative-thinking, planning, and problem-solving skills.

The child can build structures with miniature marshmallows, using the toothpicks to hold joints together. The structures can be towers, castles, people, creatures, or abstract objects. For a variation, combine large and small marshmallows, use colored marshmallows, or use peanut butter instead of toothpicks for glue!

ONCE UPON A PROP

Spark cooperative tale-telling with
a bagful of commonplace props.

WHAT YOU'LL NEED: Large bag or pillowcase filled with 6 to 10 common items (sock, spoon, rock, pencil, etc.)

OBJECTIVE: Child will use problem-solving, creative-thinking, and language skills.

Fill a bag or pillowcase with a small assortment of commonplace items. The child can help choose the items. When the story bag is ready, reach into the bag and, without looking, choose one of the items. Begin a story using the prop as part of the plot! Then invite the child to take a turn, closing his or her eyes, picking a prop, and then making up the next part of the story, weaving the prop into the story. Continue taking turns picking a prop and adding it to the story until the last prop is chosen, signaling time to make up the story ending (which includes the last prop, of course).

ROCK & CLAY CREATURES AND THINGS

Turn rocks into creatures with features using a little bit of clay.

WHAT YOU'LL NEED: Rocks, stones, plasticine clay, cardboard

OBJECTIVE: Child will use creative-thinking and problem-solving skills.

The child can create animals, people, Martians, and monsters out of rocks using clay to add features or to hold smaller pebbles in place. The clay can be used to create legs, horns, eyes, ears, tails, or anything the child can think up. The creatures can be made to lay flat on cardboard or to stand on their own. To simplify the activity, invite the child to explore creating rock sculptures combining the clay with rocks to make interesting shapes, unusual things, and pretty designs.

WHEEL ALONG

Find two wheels and a pole, and explore how things roll!

WHAT YOU'LL NEED: Plasticine clay, assorted household items for wheels and axles (pencils, straws, thread spools, paper plates, plastic coffee can lids)

OBJECTIVE: Child will problem solve, plan, execute, and test out ideas.

The child can experiment with wheels and axles using common household items. Gather assorted items together to get the child started. The child can choose which things to use for wheels and what to use for the axle and can then secure the wheels to the axle with plasticine. The child can create two or three different kinds of wheels and axles and experiment to see which vehicles roll better, farther, and fastest.

121 ODDS AND ENDS WEAVING

Weave together a medley of things for fun and display!

 WHAT YOU'LL NEED: Burlap fabric, scissors, yarn, ribbon, string, blunt darning needle, nature items (feathers, twigs, thin leaves, etc.). Optional: Cardboard

OBJECTIVE: Child will make decisions and use creative-thinking skills.

The child can cut pieces of yarn, ribbon, and string, and weave them in and out of burlap using the blunt darning needle. Nature items can also be collected to weave into the burlap, creating an abstract weaving out of found and collected objects. For easier weaving, make a loom out of cardboard by notching the edges on either end. Wrap a piece of yarn around the board through the notches and then tie it tightly in the back to create the loom. More notches can be spaced closer together or fewer notches farther apart to make it easier or more challenging for the child to weave ribbons, yarn, and string over and under the yarn strings. The child can use fingers instead of a darning needle with the cardboard loom. Found objects such as feathers and twigs can also be woven into this loom.

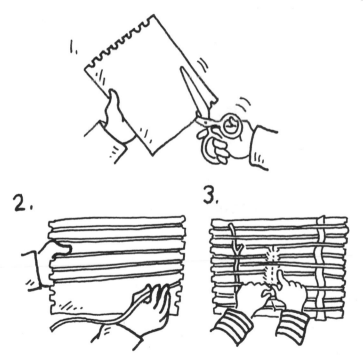

122 CREASE, CRUMPLE, CRIMP & CURL

Fold and fashion fanciful paper strip sculptures.

 WHAT YOU'LL NEED: Construction paper, scissors, unsharpened pencil, nontoxic white glue, tape. Optional: Hole punch, nontoxic glitter glue, yarn

OBJECTIVE: Child will use creative thinking to explore, plan, and construct.

 Provide a paper base and an assortment of precut construction paper strips in a variety of colors. Encourage the child to try different ways to use the paper to create a three-dimensional sculpture. The paper can be bent or folded. It can be pleated or crimped. Wrap it around a pencil to curl it. The ends can be fringed. The child can use glue or tape to attach the strips to the paper base. For variation and intrigue, add a hole punch, nontoxic glitter glue, and yarn to the supplies!

DANCE STREAMERS 123

Swirl and sway with streamers, and dance away!

 WHAT YOU'LL NEED: 2 plastic lids, scissors, crepe paper rolls. Optional: Music

OBJECTIVE: Child will explore creative movement.

The child can hold and wave dance streamers, using them to explore movement and dance. To make the dance streamers, cut the centers out of two plastic lids so they are hoops; be sure there are no sharp edges. The child can help tie several long strips (two to three feet) of crepe paper onto each hoop. The child can use the streamers, holding one in each hand, or experiment with movement using just one. Encourage the child to try different kinds of movements. The child can move slow or fast, with big movements or little ones. For greater challenge, add music to the mix!

124

SHAPE, PAINT, AND BAKE COOKIES

Make captivating cookies that are lovely to look at and tasty to eat.

WHAT YOU'LL NEED: Purchased sugar-cookie dough or your favorite recipe already prepared, rolling pin, cookie cutters, 2 egg yolks, 4 small containers, food coloring, clean brush, cookie sheet, spatula, pot holders, timer. Optional: Raisins, chocolate morsels

OBJECTIVE: Child will follow steps in a process and observe (and taste!) changes.

Wash hands first! When cookie dough is ready, have the child help you roll it out and cut out shapes with cookie cutters. Now it's time to paint the cookies! Make cookie paint by mixing the egg yolks with a little water and dividing it into four containers. Add a drop or two of food coloring to each container. Invite the child to paint the cookies before baking. For a variation, add a topping, such as chocolate morsels or raisins. Follow the recipe directions and bake!

The most instructive experiences are those of everyday life.
Friedrich Nietzsche

LEAF PRINTING

125

Remember and record lovely leaves with painted prints.

 WHAT YOU'LL NEED: Different types of leaves, poster or tempera paint, brush, paper, paper towel, rolling pin

OBJECTIVE: Child will observe, compare, and record.

The child can paint the underside of a leaf and then place it, paint side down, on paper. Place a paper towel on top of the leaf, and have the child gently roll the rolling pin over the paper towel and leaf to make the print. Then lift the paper towel and leaf carefully. Try this with a few different types of leaves and have the child examine them. How are the leaves the same? How are they different? Which leaf is the prettiest?

126

ROLLER PAINTING

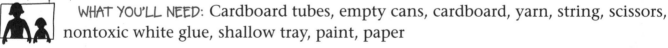

Create a paint roller and roll out a painting.

 WHAT YOU'LL NEED: Cardboard tubes, empty cans, cardboard, yarn, string, scissors, nontoxic white glue, shallow tray, paint, paper

OBJECTIVE: Child will predict, experiment, and observe.

The child can use assorted cylinders to make a variety of rollers and then print with each of them and compare the printed results. Remove the labels from the cans. The child can make rollers by gluing cardboard shapes onto the empty cans; by gluing pieces of string or yarn on an empty can or cardboard tube; and by cutting or punching holes in a cardboard tube. After the glue is dry, dip finished rollers in a tray of diluted paint and roll them on paper to make designs.

WOOD SCRAP SCULPTURE

127

*Build and construct creative sculptures
with wood scraps.*

WHAT YOU'LL NEED: Newspaper, wood scraps (often free at lumberyards), nontoxic white glue, sandpaper, plastic goggles, tempera paint, brush

OBJECTIVE: Child will use creative-thinking and problem-solving skills.

Start by spreading newspaper over the construction area. Gather together all the wood pieces so the child can sort through and choose just the right ones (the adult should check the wood for splinters). Provide sandpaper and goggles so the child can sand the wood if he or she would like to. The child can then glue wood pieces together to make an abstract or symbolic sculpture. When the glue has dried, the child can choose to paint the sculpture or can leave it natural.

128

CAN YOU SEE MY FACE?

*Turn twigs and leaves and odds and ends
into found faces!*

WHAT YOU'LL NEED: Paper, assorted household and nature objects (bottle caps, buttons, rubber bands, twigs, leaves, etc.)

OBJECTIVE: Child will use problem-solving skills, and creative and symbolic thinking.

Gather assorted natural and household items. Challenge the child to arrange items on a piece of paper to create a face. To make it easier to begin, suggest the child start by picking an item to use for a nose and ask the child where to place it on the paper. If the child has difficulty, have him or her look at the shape and position of your nose! After that it's a simple matter of picking eyes and a mouth. Other features can also be added. After a face is finished, take turns making changes by replacing parts of the face with different items.

GEOBOARD

129

Make shape art, then take it apart!

WHAT YOU'LL NEED: Piece of wood, nails, hammer, large colored rubber bands. Optional: Ribbon, yarn

OBJECTIVE: Child will explore and observe geometric shapes and relationships.

Make a geoboard for the child by hammering large nails at equal intervals (about 1½ inches) in rows on a board. The child can help (with supervision) with some of the nailing. When the board is complete, the child can then make geometric designs by looping the large rubber bands around the nails (be sure you are using rubber bands large enough so the child isn't frustrated and they are safe—the band won't pop off and hurt the child). For an easier, more freeform variation, nail 8 to 15 large nails randomly on a wooden base. The child can use ribbons and yarn and weave them around the nails to make designs.

DOT PAINTING

130

Dab with dots to create colorful painted point mosaics.

WHAT YOU'LL NEED: Tempera paint, fruit foam trays, paper, cotton swabs

OBJECTIVE: Child will explore and experiment.

The child can use cotton swabs to make dot pictures. Pour several colors of tempera paint into well-washed fruit foam trays for easy dipping. The child can dip the swabs into paint and then dab them onto paper to create dot pictures. For a variation, provide unusual color combinations. The child might explore dot painting using white dots on black construction paper, or blue and yellow dots on yellow paper, or various shades of pink on red paper!

PUDDING PAINTING

131

Finger paint with pudding, and eat the paint, too!

WHAT YOU'LL NEED: Instant pudding, milk, bowl, measuring cup, electric mixer, foil

OBJECTIVE: Child will use senses to explore self-expression.

Have child wash hands first! Then prepare the box of instant pudding together with the child. Place a sheet of foil on top of a clean table. Scoop out a cupful of the pudding mix onto the foil. The child can finger paint with the pudding on top of the foil.

132

I'M ON TV

Talk on TV and pretend the whole world can see!

WHAT YOU'LL NEED: Cardboard box, scissors, paint, brush, nontoxic white glue, buttons or bottle caps. Optional: Toilet paper tube, yarn, foil

OBJECTIVE: Child will use language skills and prior knowledge to communicate ideas.

Make a TV out of a cardboard carton. The adult can cut a "viewing screen" out of the front and back of a box. The child can then paint and decorate the box. The child may want to paint the TV black or brown or create a rainbow or scenic TV box—honor all choices! Knobs can be painted on the box, or the child may want to glue on buttons or bottle caps. The child can also make a microphone by painting a toilet paper tube and gluing a length of yarn to the bottom and a ball of foil to the top. When the box is dry, set it on its side on a table. The child stands behind the box so his or her face is seen in the TV screen. The child can then use the microphone and broadcast news of the house.

ANIMAL PANTOMIME

133

Act out animal movements for a beastly guessing game.

 WHAT YOU'LL NEED: Paper bag, animal pictures, index cards, nontoxic white glue. Optional: Markers or crayons

OBJECTIVE: Child will use creative-thinking and problem-solving skills to communicate ideas.

Glue on or draw pictures of various animals on index cards. Place cards in a bag and take turns pulling one out. The person who has chosen a card peeks at it and then places it face-down outside the bag. That person then pantomimes the action of the animal for the other player to guess. If the other player is having trouble figuring out what the animal is, use animal sounds for clues!

134 # TELL A TALE ON FELT

Create characters and creatures for spellbinding tale-telling.

WHAT YOU'LL NEED: Felt board, old magazines, construction paper, scissors, sandpaper, nontoxic white glue. Optional: Markers or crayons

OBJECTIVE: Child will use creative-thinking and language skills.

The child can go through old magazines and tear out pictures of people and animals, glue them on construction paper to make them sturdy, cut them out, and glue a strip of sandpaper on the back to create felt board storytelling characters. The sandpaper allows the character to stick onto a felt board. The child can place the characters on a felt board and make up and tell stories with them. For more difficulty, the child can draw pictures on construction paper to make the characters, and these characters can be included in the felt-board troupe. When any of the pieces get worn or torn, new characters can be created and added.

135

DANGER! VOLCANO EXPLOSION AREA!

▼▼▼▼▼▼▼▼▼▼▼▼▼▼▼▼▼▼▼▼▼▼▼▼▼▼▼▼▼▼▼▼▼

Create bubbling, fizzy explosions for dramatic science play.

 WHAT YOU'LL NEED: Sand or dirt, empty can, vinegar, baking soda, food coloring. Optional: Water, milk, lemonade

OBJECTIVE: Child will experiment and observe.

The child can make a volcanic mountain out of sand or dirt in a sand table or in an outside play area. Help the child place an empty can, open end up, in the top of the mountain. The child can then fill the can halfway with vinegar and add a few drops of food coloring. Then add a spoonful of baking soda. Watch the eruption! Talk with the child about chemical reactions and share the information that when baking soda is mixed with an acid it causes a reaction (creating the carbon dioxide "explosion"). The child might want to experiment further (with adult supervision) to discover other liquids that will have the same effect when mixed with baking soda. The child can try putting a spoonful of baking soda into a half cup each of water, milk, and lemonade to see what the results are.

Learning is a treasure that will follow its owner everywhere.
Chinese proverb

136 TISSUE PAPER PAINTING

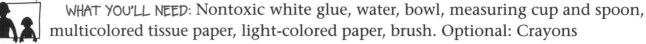

Create brilliantly colored collages from tissue paper pieces.

WHAT YOU'LL NEED: Nontoxic white glue, water, bowl, measuring cup and spoon, multicolored tissue paper, light-colored paper, brush. Optional: Crayons

OBJECTIVE: Child will use creative-thinking skills for self-expression.

Make a diluted glue mixture (1 cup of water with 2 tablespoons of glue mixed in). Cut or tear colored tissue paper into small pieces. The child can choose paper pieces and arrange them on paper. Then the child paints them in place using the diluted glue mixture. The colors will mix and blend as they are painted with the liquid. For a variation, the child can draw a picture on the paper first and then add the tissue paper to decorate the picture.

SPOON A PING-PONG ALONG 137

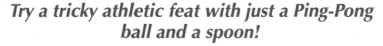

Try a tricky athletic feat with just a Ping-Pong ball and a spoon!

WHAT YOU'LL NEED: Ping-Pong ball, tablespoon

OBJECTIVE: Child will use gross-motor and problem-solving skills.

Challenge the child to carry a Ping-Pong ball in a spoon across a room without dropping it. This is not easy to do and may take some practice! After the child has mastered the task, make it even trickier. How fast can the child carry the ball across the room without dropping it? Can the child carry it while weaving around several chairs instead of straight across the room? Create a simple obstacle course with the child to test the child's Ping-Pong ball skill!

138

GLUE DROPS

Turn glue blobs into unique individual thingamabobs!

 WHAT YOU'LL NEED: Nontoxic white or colored glue, markers, wax paper, yarn, nail

OBJECTIVE: Child will use creative-thinking skills and observe changes.

The child can squeeze glue out into various large, odd-shaped globs on wax paper. Put the wax paper in a safe place to allow the glue to dry. (Depending on how big the glue blobs are, they can take up to a day or two to dry.) When dry, the child can decorate the blobs with markers. The hard decorated blobs can then be easily removed from the paper. An adult can punch holes with a nail so the child can string the blobs on yarn to make a necklace or a window hanging!

ONE BOWL OF ICE CREAM, PLEASE!

139

Mix up a simple recipe of ice cream for one!

 WHAT YOU'LL NEED: ½ cup whipping cream, 2 tablespoons powdered sugar, ½ teaspoon vanilla, measuring cups and spoons, spoon, cup, plastic wrap

OBJECTIVE: Child will follow directions, measure, and observe changes.

Wash hands before beginning! The child can measure the whipping cream, powdered sugar, and vanilla into a cup, stir the mixture with a spoon, cover it with plastic, and put it in the freezer. After a few hours the ice cream will be ready to eat!

140 OCEAN IN A BOTTLE

Make an ocean and watch the waves tumble and twirl.

WHAT YOU'LL NEED: Clear plastic bottle, funnel, salad oil, water, food coloring, superglue. Optional: Plastic pitcher, glitter, fish charms

OBJECTIVE: Child will experiment and observe changes.

The child can use a funnel to carefully fill a clean, clear, empty plastic bottle approximately a third full with salad oil. The child can then use the sink or a plastic pitcher to add water almost to the top. Have the child add a few drops of food coloring. Glitter and fish charms can also be included to make the ocean more lively! Screw the top on and tightly secure it (adult can add some superglue so the ocean won't accidentally overflow). Now the ocean is ready to roll! The child can place the bottle on its side and gently roll it back and forth to watch the waves form and dance.

141 BUILDING BREAD

Bake dainty delicious little loaves of beautiful bread.

WHAT YOU'LL NEED: 1 package yeast, 1 cup lukewarm water, 1 teaspoon sugar, 1 teaspoon salt, 2 cups flour, 1 tablespoon oil, bowl, measuring cups and spoons, wooden board, extra flour, clean towel, cookie sheet, pot holders, timer. Optional: Loaf pan

OBJECTIVE: Child will follow steps in a process, measure, and observe changes.

Wash hands first! Collect all the ingredients in a clean working area. The child can help measure the water, sugar, and yeast into a bowl and mix it. After the yeast has dissolved (a couple minutes), the child can measure and add 1 cup of flour, and mix again. Add the salt, oil, and second cup of flour and mix; the bread is ready for kneading. Sprinkle a wooden board or clean working area with flour and take turns kneading the dough (about five minutes). Then put the dough back in the bowl, cover it with a clean towel, and set it in a warm corner to rise (about 45 minutes). Encourage the child to peek under the cover every now and again to observe the rising. When the dough is ready, it can be divided into small balls to be molded and baked on a cookie sheet (about 15 minutes at 400 degrees). Or the child can model one small ball into a personal loaf for quick baking, and the rest can be put into a greased loaf pan and baked for 45 minutes at 375 degrees.

If children grew up according to early indicators, we should have nothing but geniuses.
Johann Wolfgang von Goethe

142

GREAT & GRAND KITCHEN BAND

Rap and tap and beat along while the music plays a rhythm song!

 WHAT YOU'LL NEED: Cassette or CD with a strong beat, assorted kitchen tools (pot covers, wooden spoons, pans, chopsticks, etc.)

OBJECTIVE: Child will use listening skills to explore rhythm and beat.

Gather together an assortment of cooking utensils for the child to create kitchen-band music. The child can explore the different items and how to make musical sounds with them. Two pot covers can be used as cymbals. A pot can be beat like a drum with a metal spoon or chopsticks. Two wooden spoons can be tapped together like rhythm sticks—let them use whichever end they want. After the child has explored the musical possibilities of the utensils, one instrument can be chosen (to start with!) to play along with a music cassette or CD. The child can sit and listen to the music, paying attention to the rhythm and the beat, and play along. For more challenge, the child can march around the room playing the instrument along to the music!

TOOL PRINTING

Create kitchen art using cooking utensils for artist's tools.

WHAT YOU'LL NEED: Shallow tray, tempera paint, common kitchen and household tools (potato masher, fork, garlic press, whisk), paper

OBJECTIVE: Child will experiment and observe.

The child can experiment with printmaking using common utensils. The child can dip the utensil into a shallow tray of paint and then press it on paper to make a print. The child can explore and observe the different print each kind of tool makes and then create designs and pictures by printing. If the child enjoys printing activities, on another day, gather together a different assortment of common items to experiment with. Other good items to start with are a comb, keys, a large paper clip, and a plastic lid.

PING-PONG ART

Paint Ping-Pong pictures!

WHAT YOU'LL NEED: Pie tin, construction paper, scissors, Ping-Pong balls, tempera paint, paint containers, spoon. Optional: Brownie pan, liquid starch

OBJECTIVE: Child will experiment, and use creative-thinking and observation skills.

Use a pie tin, paper circle, Ping-Pong ball, and paint to create circle designs. Cut a construction paper circle the size of the pie tin base and place it in the pie tin. The child can dip the Ping-Pong ball into the paint, use a spoon to lift it out, and drop the ball into the pie tin. The child can then jiggle the pie tin to create a design with the rolling ball. For a variation, use a brownie pan for square designs. Add a second Ping-Pong ball and a second color of paint for more fun! For thicker paint consistency, add some liquid starch to the paint.

USING MY POWERS— REFLECTING!

When children play, they are learning. Their daily experiences and explorations offer them the opportunity to develop a full range of thinking skills. They are constantly gathering new information, applying and analyzing what they learn, and putting findings together to construct meaning for themselves. Children naturally reflect on their experiences and discoveries, using what they know and what they are learning to grow in understanding. They are natural problem-solvers. This chapter provides a wide range of activities and experiences that allow for reflection, which offers the opportunity for children to hone their inherent skills as problem-solvers and to develop confidence in their own powers.

145 ADVICE FOR MOTHER GOOSE

Help Mother Goose with her plentiful perplexities and problems!

WHAT YOU'LL NEED: Mother Goose nursery rhymes book

OBJECTIVE: Child will use critical-thinking and problem-solving skills.

Share one or two nursery rhymes with the child. After listening to a rhyme, the child can describe and tell about the difficulties that the characters are involved in. Encourage the child then to suggest ideas that the characters might try (if they could) to solve each of their problems, or if it's too late, what they might have done to prevent them!

Jack Be Nimble

ALIKE & UNALIKE

146

Tell what's the same and what's not!

WHAT YOU'LL NEED: Household items (salt and pepper shakers, sock and shoe, spoon and fork, etc.)

OBJECTIVE: Child will use critical-thinking skills.

Take turns finding and telling one similarity and one difference for two items. The adult can start the game by suggesting two different items and challenging the child to name a way they are alike and a way they are not alike. Begin with easy matches such as a shoe and a sock, salt and pepper shakers, a spoon and a fork. As the child becomes familiar with the game, take turns thinking up two items to pose to one another. Increase the challenge as you go by choosing items whose similarities are not so easily visible, for example, a bucket and a sponge, or a pencil and a computer.

147

MAKING AN IMPRESSION

Use playdough to make a good impression!

WHAT YOU'LL NEED: Playdough, variety of tools for impression making (toothpicks, buttons, fork, empty cans, penny, rock, key, small toys, potato masher, leaves, etc.)

OBJECTIVE: Child will experiment and make observations.

The child can explore impression making using different kinds of household objects. Gather an assortment of items for the child to press into the playdough to make impressions. After experimenting, the child can search for other objects that might make interesting indentations. The child can explore the various impressions each item makes, create impression designs, or even make impression patterns using the tools. Discuss the shapes and impressions with the child.

PHOTOJOURNALISM

Record an adventure with pictures and words.

WHAT YOU'LL NEED: Disposable camera, construction paper, nontoxic white glue, marker, clear contact paper, hole punch, ring binder or report folder

OBJECTIVE: Child will use critical-thinking, problem-solving, and language skills.

The child can use a disposable camera to take photographs of a park exploration, a walk to the store, or a visit from a friend (all with adult supervision). After the photos have been developed, the child can choose which ones tell the most about the visit, walk, or adventure. Have the child glue each of the chosen pictures on a separate sheet of construction paper. The child can then dictate picture labels to describe the events. Cover the pages with clear contact paper, and use a hole punch to make holes on the edge of the pages. The pages can be placed in a ring binder or report folder to create a photojournal of the experience.

What we have to learn to do, we learn by doing.
Aristotle

RHYME BOX

149

Rhyme with real things!

 WHAT YOU'LL NEED: Shoe box, 4 to 8 pairs of small objects that rhyme (fork/cork, block/rock, ring/string, duck [toy]/truck [toy], jar [plastic]/car [toy], box/socks)

OBJECTIVE: Child will use auditory discrimination.

Create a rhyme box filled with pairs of real objects that rhyme. Gather up four to eight rhyming pairs and place them in a shoe box. Invite the child to explore the items in the box and talk about the name of each item. Then play a rhyming game together. The child closes his or her eyes and reaches into the box and pulls out an item. The child looks at the item, names it, and then checks the box to find the rhyming partner. The child takes it out of the box also. Then the adult takes a turn. Continue playing until all the rhyming partners have been found and put together. The child can also spread out all the items in the box and work independently to match up the pairs.

150

CAN YOU TIPPLEFIZZY ME?

Play a word detective game.

OBJECTIVE: Child will use listening and critical-thinking skills.

One person chooses a common word (water, cat, shoes) to keep a secret for the other to guess. "Tipplefizzy" is substituted for the word and used in sentences in place of the secret word (I'm thirsty, I want a glass of tipplefizzy.) Tipplefizzy is used in as many different sentences as possible until the other person can guess what word tipplefizzy is being used for!

151 WHAT DOES IT MEAN?

Listen and listen again to find a word's meaning!

OBJECTIVE: Child will use critical-thinking and listening skills.

Choose a word or word phrase that the child is not familiar with for this sleuthing game. Tell the child the word but not its meaning. Then use the word in a sentence that gives a clue to the meaning of the word. Continue to make up new sentences using the word in different ways until the child is able to figure out what it means! Start off with easy words or word phrases (for example, supper, stocking). Increase the difficulty by using less concrete words, but words that the context will give strong clues to (lazy).

TORN-PAPER PICTURES 152

*Make beautiful paper pictures using only
colored paper and glue.*

WHAT YOU'LL NEED: Construction paper, nontoxic white glue. Optional: Wrapping paper, tissue paper

OBJECTIVE: Child will use creative-thinking and problem-solving skills.

The child can make decorative collage designs by tearing construction paper into big and little shapes. Help the child discover the technique that works best for tearing paper by encouraging experimentation with thumb positioning. For a variation, include wrapping paper and tissue paper. For further exploration, share with the child pictures that artists have made using torn paper. Some children's book illustrators who use torn paper are Patricia Mullins and Candace Whitman. Some illustrators who cut paper and use it as part of their collage art are Ezra Jack Keats and Eric Carle.

LEGENDARY LISTS

153

*Invent fanciful categories and fill them
with imaginary listings.*

OBJECTIVE: Child will use critical- and creative-thinking skills.

Take turns creating categories and challenging one another to name real or pretend events, ideas, or items that fit into them. Encourage the child to have fun and be creative when making the list! Some examples of categories that you might suggest for one another are: Important items to take along on a trip to Mars; new holidays that should be invented; unusual ways to use a paper cup; new flavors of ice cream that might be created. For further fun, turn a fanciful list into a fiction story!

154 # ONE-PIECE PUZZLE MATCH

Mix and match one-piece puzzles and parts.

WHAT YOU'LL NEED: Construction paper, scissors, two large manila envelopes

OBJECTIVE: Child will use observation and problem-solving skills.

The child or adult can create several one-piece puzzles by folding construction paper in half and cutting or tearing a shape out of the center of each of the papers. Using the same color paper for all the puzzles, make three to eight one-piece puzzles. (Make three for a toddler, more for an older child.) Place all the center pieces into one pile and mix them up, and put all the puzzle frames into a second pile and mix them up! The child can try to fit the centers into the frames by finding the middle part that fits. Store frames and holes in two separate envelopes.

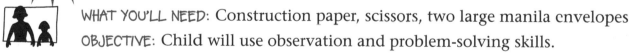

PUZZLE PEEKER

155

Turn pictures into puzzles with a puzzle peeker.

WHAT YOU'LL NEED: Picture from a book or magazine, paper, scissors

OBJECTIVE: Child will use observation and critical-thinking skills.

Make a puzzle peeker by cutting five to eight horizontal strips in a piece of paper to about an inch and a half from the edge. The puzzle peeker is placed on top of a mystery picture. The child pulls one strip back at a time and tries to guess what the picture is. To increase the challenge, place the puzzle peeker on top of a complex picture!

156

JUST LIKE ME

Look and see what's the same as me!

WHAT YOU'LL NEED: Magazines

OBJECTIVE: Child will use critical-thinking and language skills.

Look through magazines together and find pictures of people to investigate. Choose one person in a picture to look at. Then invite the child to tell something about that person that is the same as the child and something that is different. For example, the child might say, "He is the same as me because he has a shirt with buttons, and I have a shirt with buttons. He is different than me because he is a grown-up, and I am a kid." Or, "She is the same as me because we both have brown hair, but we are different because she is outside, and I am inside." After the child has taken a turn, take a turn yourself! For a variation, play the game outside while taking a walk, at a park, or even while watching TV. Note passersby or TV characters, and take turns quickly thinking of ways they are the same as or different than each of you.

WHAT WEIGHS MORE?

Compare weights with a simple sock test!

WHAT YOU'LL NEED: Variety of small household objects and toys, two large socks, balance scale (see activity 48) or long block and a piece of heavy cardboard

OBJECTIVE: Child will experiment, compare, and draw conclusions.

The child can test the comparative weights of two objects using two socks to test by feel. The child chooses two different objects to test, predicts which is the heaviest and which is the lightest, and then puts each item into a separate sock. Standing up and holding a sock in each hand, the child tests the weight by feel. To check the results of the sock test, the child can use a balance scale or can make a simple balance beam by resting a piece of cardboard on a block. For a further challenge, the child can test four or five items to find out which is the heaviest. To determine the heaviest item, the child tests two items at a time, each time eliminating the lightest, and testing the heavier item with the next item from the group of five. Through testing, the child will eliminate the four lightest items one by one and will end up with the heaviest item.

Ah! not in knowledge is happiness but in the acquisition of knowledge.
Edgar Allan Poe

158

ROLL POLL

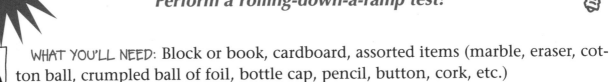

Perform a rolling-down-a-ramp test!

WHAT YOU'LL NEED: Block or book, cardboard, assorted items (marble, eraser, cotton ball, crumpled ball of foil, bottle cap, pencil, button, cork, etc.)

OBJECTIVE: Child will predict, test, and draw conclusions.

Gather up assorted items for the roll poll. The child can make a ramp for the testing by elevating one end of a piece of cardboard on a block or book. The child can then predict which of the assembled items will roll and which will not. The items can be tested one by one to check out the predictions. The child can then sort the items into two groups: things that roll and things that don't roll. Encourage the child to discuss and conclude what the difference is. (Adult needs to supervise—smaller objects can be choking hazards!)

159

ME BOX

Create a box of items that together tell a personal tale.

WHAT YOU'LL NEED: Box, assorted items chosen by child

OBJECTIVE: Child will use creative- and critical-thinking skills.

Challenge the child to assemble a "Me Box." The child can choose and place five or six personal items inside the box. Encourage the child to pick things that together will tell something important about him or her. After the box is created, the child can share it with family members and explain all the choices.

SPLASH COMPARISONS

160

Splash rocks in water and compare the splashes!

 WHAT YOU'LL NEED: Large piece of paper with concentric circles drawn on it, large plastic bowl filled with water, rocks of varying sizes. Optional: Yarn, scissors

OBJECTIVE: Child will predict, test, and draw conclusions.

This is an outdoor activity! The child can gather big (but not too big!) and little rocks for splash testing. After the rocks have been assembled, place a large plastic bowl filled with water (outside) in the middle of the sheet of paper. The child can drop rocks, one by one, from the same height (arm straight out above bowl). After each rock is dropped, the child can mark the farthest splash of that rock by placing the rock on the splash. After all the rocks have been tested, the child can evaluate the splash capabilities by viewing how far each rock is sitting from the bowl. For a further challenge, the child can measure and cut a length of yarn the distance from the bowl to the farthest splash of each rock, and then comparing the pieces of yarn.

161

WHERE IS IT?

Puzzle about places with a place guessing game.

 OBJECTIVE: Child will use listening, speaking, and critical-thinking skills.

Take turns thinking up different places to use for puzzling one another. One person thinks of a place and tells all about what kinds of things people do at that place. The other person guesses what the place is. (For example, the park, the circus, a church, a swimming pool, etc.) For a variation, pantomime what people do at the place!

GUESSTIMATING AROUND THE HOUSE

162

• •

Turn everyday experiences into estimating opportunities!

OBJECTIVE: Child will estimate, check estimates, and count.

Challenge the child to make guesstimates (estimating guesses) around the home. The child can make a prediction and then test it out. For example, ask the child to guesstimate how many steps it is from the bed to the closet, how many white shoes are in the child's closet, or how many toothbrushes are in the bathroom. Then go with the child to check the guesstimates!

163

SHAPE CONCENTRATION

– –

Play a concentration game and search for hidden shape pairs.

WHAT YOU'LL NEED: Index cards, scissors, markers. Optional: Stickers

OBJECTIVE: Child will use visual memory, matching, and shape recognition.

Prepare a concentration game by cutting index cards into squares and then drawing pairs of shapes on separate cards. Make 8 to 16 cards (two of each shape). To play shape concentration, mix up all the cards and spread them out face down. One person turns over two cards, hoping to find a match. If the cards match, the person takes the pair and gets a second turn. If the two cards do not match, the cards are turned face down again and the next person takes a turn. Play until all the pairs have been found. The person with the most cards is the winner. For a variation, make different kinds of concentration games using stickers (animal concentration, dinosaur concentration, butterfly concentration, etc.).

PAPER WEAVING

164

Create woven art with colorful paper strips and a paper loom.

WHAT YOU'LL NEED: Construction paper, scissors

OBJECTIVE: Child will explore concepts of over and under to make a pattern.

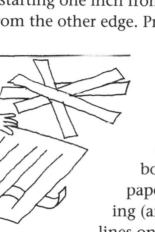

Make the paper loom with construction paper by cutting eight parallel slits starting one inch from one edge of the paper and ending one inch from the other edge. Prepare the weaving strips by cutting strips of construction paper in different colors. The child can weave the strips over and under the rows on the paper loom. For a more decorative weaving, cut the weaving strips from a wallpaper sample book. (Many wallpaper stores will give away books that contain samples of discontinued papers.) To make the weaving more challenging (and to give it a pop art effect), cut curvy lines on the loom instead of straight ones.

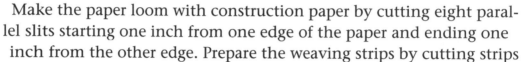

Grown-ups never understand anything for themselves, and it is tiresome for children to be always and forever explaining things to them.

Antoine de Saint-Exupéry

PRETTY PASTA PATTERNS

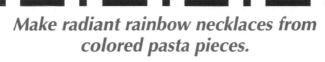

Make radiant rainbow necklaces from colored pasta pieces.

WHAT YOU'LL NEED: Assorted pasta with holes, food coloring, rubbing alcohol, plastic self-sealing bags, aluminum foil, yarn, masking tape. Optional: Construction paper, cardboard, nontoxic white glue

OBJECTIVE: Child will make patterns.

The child can help color the pasta and then use it to make patterned necklaces and decorations. Invite the child to place a handful of pasta in a plastic bag and add a few drops of food coloring. The adult adds a small amount of rubbing alcohol. (The alcohol will help create brilliant colors and will also help the pasta dry evenly.) Seal the bag and ask the child to shake it so all the pasta pieces get colored. Spread the pasta out on aluminum foil to dry. Make several different colors of each of the pasta shapes. When all the pasta has dried, the child can create necklaces or decorations by stringing the colored pasta in different patterns on the yarn. (Wrap the end of the piece of yarn with masking tape to make stringing easier.) For a variation, the child can make pattern pictures by gluing the colored pasta in pattern rows on strips of construction paper or gluing pasta in designs on paper or cardboard to make pasta mosaics.

It is not the answer that enlightens, but the question.
Eugène Ionesco

WHAT'S THE QUESTION?

166

Reveal the answer and guess the question!

 OBJECTIVE: Child will use creative- and critical-thinking skills.

Turn questioning and answering backward and make it into a game. Take turns making up and reporting "answers" to one another. After one person makes up an answer, the other person comes up with a question for which the answer given could be true. To make the game more challenging, try coming up with three different questions for which the answer could be true! To simplify, choose answers that the child commonly uses in replying to questions, such as the child's name, the child's age, or "fine."

167

STRING PAINTING

Use a common object to obtain uncommon art!

WHAT YOU'LL NEED: Several colors of tempera paint, containers, lengths of string, paper, newspaper

OBJECTIVE: Child will experiment and observe.

The child can achieve a variety of different effects using a string dipped in paint as a painting tool. Spread newspaper on the work area. The child can place a piece of string in one of the paint containers and allow the string to soak up the paint. The child then arranges the string on the paper, folds the paper in half, and pulls the string through

the folded paper. Pulling the string will create a design. Through experimentation, the child will discover that the design result can be varied by how the string is placed on the paper and also by how it is pulled. A second and third string soaked in different colors can be used on the same paper to create blended effects.

168

FOLD AND SEE, SYMMETRY!

Make symmetrical paint pictures.

WHAT YOU'LL NEED: Construction paper, tempera paint, small containers, spoons

OBJECTIVE: Child will use observation skills to explore symmetry.

Help the child fold a paper in half and then open it up. The child then scoops one or two spoonfuls of paint into the middle of the paper and folds it in half again along the crease. The child gently pats and smooths the closed paper before opening it once more to discover the symmetrical design. After observing the colorful design, encourage the child to notice and talk about the two identical shapes that have been created. For a variation, the child can make symmetrical picture designs by using two or three colors at one time!

TOUCHING THE OUTSIDE

169

Turn a nature collection into a touch-and-guess game.

WHAT YOU'LL NEED: Cardboard, nontoxic white glue, natural items with different textures (tree bark, pine needles, dry grass, pebbles, twigs). Optional: Paper, pencil or chalk

OBJECTIVE: Child will use critical-thinking skills and tactile discrimination.

Take a walk outside together, and collect a variety of nature items. Collect two of each item! When you return, have the child glue each item to an individual piece of cardboard. After the glue has dried, with eyes closed, the child can touch each item and guess what it is by feel. The child can also match the pairs, finding the same items using touch only.

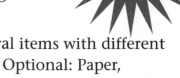

ANIMAL BINGO

Play bingo and try for three animal matches all in a row!

WHAT YOU'LL NEED: Tagboard or cardboard from cereal boxes, scissors, ruler, markers, animal stickers, large buttons, paper bag

OBJECTIVE: Child will use observation and critical-thinking skills.

Bingo boards can be made by cutting squares (approximately 8×8 inches each) out of tagboard or empty cereal boxes. With markers, draw grids on the boards to create nine squares. Use animals stickers and place a picture of a different animal in each square except the middle one. Draw a star or sun or happy face in the middle square—it is a free space. Make the game cards by cutting smaller individual cards and placing one animal sticker on each card. Use large buttons for the place markers. To play, place all the game cards in a bag. Each person starts off by putting a place marker on the free middle square. The caller then starts

the game by taking a card from the bag. The caller looks at the picture and names the animal. Each player checks their board to see if they have a picture of that animal on it. If the animal is there, the player puts a place marker on the picture. The first person to get three markers all in a row shouts "BINGO!" and is the winner. To make the game more challenging, instead of naming the animal on the card, the caller makes the sound that animal makes!

INSECTS AND SPIDERS

Make playdough bugs with lots of little legs.

WHAT YOU'LL NEED: Playdough, pipe cleaners, buttons, beans, toothpicks

OBJECTIVE: Child will count, categorize, and use creative-thinking skills.

The child can create insects and spiders by shaping the playdough and counting the body parts (two for spiders, three for insects). Pipe cleaners or toothpicks can be used for legs. The child can count just the right number of legs to make accurate bug replicas—insects have six legs and spiders have eight—or children can invent many-legged creatures. Buttons or beans can be used for eyes, dots, and decorations. (Smaller children need supervision—buttons and beans are choking hazards!) The child uses the playdough to form familiar insects and spiders or, instead, to create amazing imaginary bugs!

To be what we are, and to become what we are capable of becoming, is the only end of life.

Robert Louis Stevenson

REBUS RECIPE

Read and follow a rebus recipe and end up eating a yummy treat.

WHAT YOU'LL NEED: Measuring cups, spoon, bowl, ½ cup peanut butter, ¼ cup honey, 2½ cups puffed wheat, rebus recipe chart (paper, marker), wax paper

OBJECTIVE: Child will interpret and follow a recipe chart and measure.

Make a rebus recipe chart for a peanut butter and puffed wheat treat that shows and tells the directions with words and pictures. After washing up, the child can make the snack! Following the picture directions, the child can measure the honey, peanut butter, and puffed wheat; mix the ingredients; roll the dough into balls; and place the balls on wax paper. Then it's time to taste the delicious treat!

MOOD MATCH

Match mood pictures of people, places, events, and things!

WHAT YOU'LL NEED: Pictures of people showing different facial expressions and pictures of places, things, or activities cut from magazines (ice cream cone, puppy, people at a beach, arm with a bandage, bed, juice spill)

OBJECTIVE: Child will categorize, match, and interpret images.

Gather an assortment of pictures cut from magazines of people expressing a variety of emotions. Gather an equal number of pictures of places, events, and things. Invite the child to match the happy, sad, frightened, or angry people with pictures that show something that might have caused the person to feel that way. Encourage the child to explain the reasoning for each of the choices.

COOKING QUESTIONS

174

What's the best way to cook an egg?

WHAT YOU'LL NEED: Egg, bowl, variety of mixing tools (hand beater, spoon, fork, whisk, jar for shaking), nonstick electric frying pan, pot holder, spatula, plate. Optional: Cheese, chopped vegetables

OBJECTIVE: Child will use creative-thinking and problem-solving skills.

Challenge the child to figure out what would taste best and try it out! After washing hands, the child can crack an egg in a bowl and experiment with different tools to figure out what mixes best. The child can then decide whether to fry the egg, make a flat omelet, or scramble the egg. The adult must supervise the child as the egg is cooked in an electric frying pan. For a variation, include cheese or chopped vegetables. Put the egg on the plate, and let the child eat it!

175

WHAT'S HAPPENING HERE?

Observe, notice, note, and discuss!

OBJECTIVE: Child will use observation, critical-thinking, and speaking skills.

Share a graphic picture from a storybook, magazine, or poster with the child. Encourage the child to look at the picture, make observations, and draw conclusions based on visual clues. Ask questions to spark discussion. Here are some discussion questions to start with: Who do you think these people are? What are they doing? What would you do if you were there? How do you think the little boy/girl/dog feels? What do you think will happen next? How can you tell? Did something like that ever happen to you? What does this picture remind you of?

176 SPOONFUL OF BEANS

Pour carefully, and guess how many beans a spoon can hold!

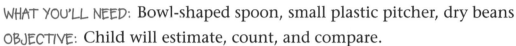

WHAT YOU'LL NEED: Bowl-shaped spoon, small plastic pitcher, dry beans

OBJECTIVE: Child will estimate, count, and compare.

The child pours dried beans from a small plastic pitcher into a bowl-shaped spoon, trying to get as many beans as possible in the spoon before any spill. As soon as the first bean spills, the child stops pouring. Observing the spoonful of beans, the child guesses how many beans are in the spoon. The spoonful of beans is then spilled out onto the table and counted to check the prediction. After counting, the child can put all the beans back into the pitcher and take a second turn—aiming for a higher number! To continue the exploration, the child can experiment by using different kinds of beans or different sizes and shapes of spoons, and comparing the results. (Adults should supervise this activity, especially with younger children. Small beans can be a choking hazard.)

What sculpture is to a block of marble, education is to a human soul.
Joseph Addison

CATEGORY COMPILATION

177

Turn category creation into a challenge game!

OBJECTIVE: Child will use classification and critical-thinking skills.

One player thinks of and names a category. The next player then tries to come up with five things that would fit in that category. Start off with familiar themes, such as colors, animals that make good pets, or yummy desserts. Increase the challenge by choosing category topics that are a little broader, such as kinds of weather, sounds animals make, kinds of shoes, etc.

178

BOX TOWER

Experiment with balance and building using boxes.

WHAT YOU'LL NEED: Large assortment of empty boxes in all different shapes and sizes (shoe box, food boxes, toothpaste box, check box, jewelry box, egg carton, milk carton, oatmeal box). Optional: Paint, brush, nontoxic white glue

OBJECTIVE: Child will experiment and use problem-solving skills.

Gather together a large assortment of boxes in a variety of sizes and shapes. The boxes can be used as is, or they can be painted ahead of time to make the building more decorative. For painted boxes, spread plenty of newspaper and invite the child to make color choices and paint each box. (A little bit of nontoxic white glue added to the paint will allow it to adhere to waxed cartons.) When the boxes are ready for building, assemble them and invite the child to explore! The child can experiment with tower creations by stacking and restacking the assortment of differently sized and shaped boxes.

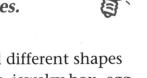

SNACK PATTERNS

179

Turn a snack treat into a tasty pattern-making feat.

 WHAT YOU'LL NEED: Celery sticks, cream cheese, spoon, paper plate, raisins, pretzel sticks. Optional: Peanuts (or other topping)

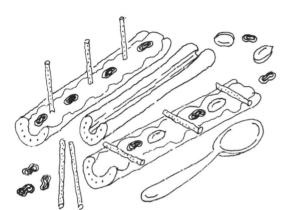

OBJECTIVE: Child will explore pattern-making.

After washing hands, the child can spread cream cheese on celery sticks with the spoon. The child can then use raisins and pretzel sticks to make pattern decorations on top. The child can make simple patterns (raisin-pretzel-raisin-pretzel-raisin-pretzel) or more complicated ones (raisin-raisin-pretzel-raisin-raisin-pretzel). A third topping (such as peanuts) can also be added to encourage more sophisticated pattern making.

COOKIE COUNTING

180

Make five raisin cookie designs!

 WHAT YOU'LL NEED: Refrigerated cookie dough, plastic knife, cookie tray, raisins, pot holders, cooling rack

OBJECTIVE: Child will count and explore number concepts.

After washing hands, the child can help cut and place cookie dough on a cookie tray. When all the cookies are placed on the tray, the child can make raisin designs on top. Challenge the child to count out and use five raisins for every cookie, but to make a different design for each cookie!

181 OVER, UNDER, AROUND, AND THROUGH

▼▼▼▼▼▼▼▼▼▼▼▼▼▼▼▼▼▼▼▼▼▼▼▼▼▼▼▼▼▼▼

Create a dot city and then draw a path over, under, and around the dot town!

WHAT YOU'LL NEED: Paper, paint, brush, markers

OBJECTIVE: Child will explore spatial concepts.

The child can make different colored dots and splotches on a large piece of paper using paint and a paintbrush. When the painting has dried, the child can use a marker to draw a path through the dot town going over, under, and around the dots and splotches. Create a challenge for the child by providing directions for the child to follow while creating the path. For example, the adult can suggest that the child go around the blue dot, under the green splotch, and above the yellow dot.

182 BLOW OR NO?

Carry out a blowing test to find out what objects are blown best.

WHAT YOU'LL NEED: Assorted small objects (crumbled aluminum foil, penny, paper clip, bottle cap), cardboard tubes, straws

OBJECTIVE: Child will predict, experiment, and draw conclusions.

Gather an assortment of small items for the blow test. (Supervise carefully—small objects may pose a choking hazard.) The child can predict which items can be moved easily by blowing and then experiment by blowing them! After testing, the child can sort the items into categories. To test further, add a cardboard tube and a straw. The child can blow through the tube and the straw to test if either changes the results.

183

BUILDING TOGETHER APART

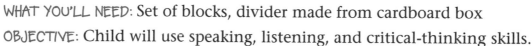

Take a "build the same building without looking" challenge!

WHAT YOU'LL NEED: Set of blocks, divider made from cardboard box

OBJECTIVE: Child will use speaking, listening, and critical-thinking skills.

Create a divider out of a large cardboard box by cutting off the flaps on both ends of a box and then cutting along the fold of two panels. The box can be set up on a table or on the floor so each person can build with blocks on one side without the other person being able to see the other's building. Divide a set of blocks so that each person (adult and child or two children) has an identical set of blocks. One person builds a building and describes each step of the building process—what kind of block is being used and where it is being placed. The other person tries to make the same building at the same time by listening to the directions and following them. When the two buildings are finished, remove the divider and compare the buildings. Then take down the buildings, put the divider back up, and reverse the roles!

Learning cannot be inherited.
Yiddish proverb

NUMBER SEARCH

184

Search for (and discover!) numbers in familiar territory!

 WHAT YOU'LL NEED: Index cards with numbers written on them

OBJECTIVE: Child will use observation skills.

Send the child on a search for a number that can be found around the house. Provide the child with a number card to make matching easy. The child can look for one number at a

time, carrying an index card with a number from 1 to 10 written on it to help the child remember just what the number looks like. Challenge the child to find that number in as many places as possible! Numbers can be found on clocks, radios, calendars, books, magazines, clothing, food boxes, etc. For a variation, have the child listen for a number, too! Numbers can be heard on the radio, on TV, in songs, and in conversations.

Happiness lies in the joy of achievement and the thrill of creative effort.

Franklin Delano Roosevelt

185 DOODLE DRAWING

Turn squiggles and lines into squirrels, lions, or designs.

WHAT YOU'LL NEED: Papers with a doodle line or shape already begun, markers or crayons

OBJECTIVE: Child will use observation and creative-thinking skills.

Draw one or two squiggles, lines, or half shapes on a piece of paper. Challenge the child to use the doodles on the paper as a picture starter. The child can turn the squiggles and lines into a picture of something or into a design. For a variation, draw two or three shapes on the paper for the child to use as a picture starter.

186 TREASURE HUNT

Find and follow clues to discover a treasure!

WHAT YOU'LL NEED: Index cards, pencil, tape, small treasure (see below)

OBJECTIVE: Child will use emergent reading skills to follow directions.

Hide a treasure (two cookies in a bag, a card that says "I Love You," a book, or a toy) somewhere in the house. Then make clue cards that lead from one place to another. Write or draw the clues on index cards to make the clue cards. The clues can be simple sentences or pictures that tell where the next clue can be found. For example, a clue card might say: "Go to a bed," "Bed," or have a picture of a bed on it. The child can go check all the beds in the house and discover the next clue card on one of them! Set each of the clue cards around the house, and tell the child where to find the first one. Use three to six clue cards to lead the child to the discovery of the treasure.

187

WHICH ONE DOESN'T GO?

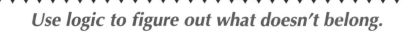

Use logic to figure out what doesn't belong.

WHAT YOU'LL NEED: Pictures cut from magazines

OBJECTIVE: Child will use critical-thinking and classification skills.

Provide the child with groups of four pictures in which one thing doesn't belong, for example: ice cream, donuts, cookies, and pizza; or sneakers, rain boots, ballet shoes, and an umbrella. Challenge the child to figure out which item doesn't belong and tell why. For further play, encourage the child to suggest a fourth item that would go with the group!

188

PICTURE PUZZLES

Make personalized puzzles to take apart and put together.

WHAT YOU'LL NEED: Picture (from a magazine, a photo of child scanned and printed out at 8×11 inches, or a drawing the child has done), stiff paper, nontoxic white glue, scissors, self-sealing plastic bag

OBJECTIVE: Child will use observation and problem-solving skills.

Have the child help choose the picture to be used. Glue the picture to a piece of stiff paper. When dry, cut the picture into three to eight odd-shaped pieces (three for a toddler, more for an older child). The child can fit the pieces together to complete the puzzle. Keep the puzzle pieces in the self-sealing bag.

MAKING MY BRAIN GROW— THINKING & EXPRESSING!

Thinking becomes powerful and language comes alive when children are able to share their ideas and see them brought to fruition. As children use words and sentences to communicate, they become able to think more deeply. As their thinking becomes richer, they spontaneously become more fluent with language and more able to express their ideas. Thinking and expressing enrich and nourish one another, and both are natural to the child. Activities and experiences that excite the child's mind and spirit are natural springboards for lively and enthusiastic thinking and expressing.

189

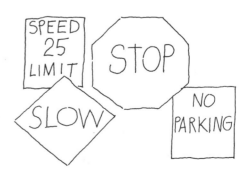

SAFE CITY

Plan a town that will keep its inhabitants safe!

WHAT YOU'LL NEED: Paper, markers, toys (cars, people, animals)

OBJECTIVE: Child will use critical-thinking and problem-solving skills.

Share ideas about what makes cities safe. Encourage the child to give reasons for ideas. The child may come up with many unique ideas as well as traditional ones. Support all ideas! Then invite the child to draw a town that incorporates some of the ideas for safety. The child can make signs, build special buildings, make parks far away from streets, etc.

190 RED, YELLOW, AND GREEN

*Perform a comparison experiment with
a tasty component.*

WHAT YOU'LL NEED: Red, yellow, and green apples; plastic knife; plate; paper towels

OBJECTIVE: Child will observe, compare, and draw conclusions.

Compare red, yellow, and green apples. Provide the apples, or visit a local market and pick them out together. Have everyone wash their hands, and be sure to wash the apples. The child can compare their shapes. Cut the apples open and compare the insides. Invite the child to notice if the inside colors are also different or if they are the same. Together, count the seeds of each apple. And finally, take a bite and talk about how the different apples taste. Encourage the child to use descriptive words, such as tart, sweet, and crunchy. For more challenge, the child can survey family members and find out which color apple is most popular.

PRINT MATCHING 191

Match assorted objects to their telltale prints!

WHAT YOU'LL NEED: Sponge, paint, shallow tray, index cards, assorted objects (large button, coins, key, comb, bottle cap)

OBJECTIVE: Child will explore, experiment, and classify.

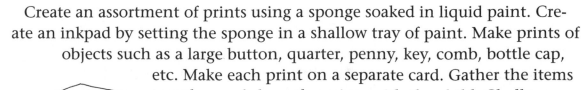

Create an assortment of prints using a sponge soaked in liquid paint. Create an inkpad by setting the sponge in a shallow tray of paint. Make prints of objects such as a large button, quarter, penny, key, comb, bottle cap, etc. Make each print on a separate card. Gather the items together and share the prints with the child. Challenge the child to match each item with its print. (Supervise the child—small objects can be choking hazards.) To continue the exploration, invite the child to make more prints!

192

SHOE SOCK SHOE SOCK SHOE SOCK

▼▼▼▼▼▼▼▼▼▼▼▼▼▼▼▼▼▼▼▼▼▼▼▼▼▼▼▼▼▼▼

Lay out a pattern for all to see!

WHAT YOU'LL NEED: Household items (such as shoes and socks, spoons and forks, etc.)

OBJECTIVE: Child will explore pattern making.

Invite the child to create patterns using household items. Make suggestions about items you can use to make patterns with; encourage the child to think up what else could be used for this activity. Patterns can be made with shoes and socks across the living room floor, spoons and forks around the kitchen table, or hats and mittens on a bed. To increase the challenge, the child can make three-part patterns.

BODY CARDS

● ●

193

Make up and perform easy or imaginative body tasks!

WHAT YOU'LL NEED: Index cards, marker

OBJECTIVE: Child will use critical-thinking skills.

Create a simple deck of body parts cards. Using ten index cards, the adult can make simple line drawings to depict different body parts: eyes, nose, mouth, head, arms, hands, legs, knees, feet, toes. Mix up the cards and then take turns picking the top one. After picking a card, make up a task for the other person to do with that body part! The tasks can be simple, for example: Clap your hands, stamp your feet, wiggle your nose. Or the tasks can be more challenging: Pick up a teddy bear with your feet, make a sound with your knees. For a variation, take two cards at a time and challenge one another with a task that involves both body parts: Put your hand on your knee.

POP-UP PUBLISHING

194

Bring books to life with pop-up people and more.

WHAT YOU'LL NEED: Paper, scissors, nontoxic white glue, crayons

OBJECTIVE: Child will use creative-thinking and language skills.

The child can help make a pop-up book by creating the pictures that will pop-up and inventing the story! To make the pop-up pages for the book, fold a paper in half. Then cut two slits in the middle of the folded paper approximately 1½ inches apart and 1½ inches long. Push the cut area to the inside to form a pop-up section. The child can draw the picture that will pop-up on another piece of paper, cut it out, and paste it onto the pop-up section. The child can also then draw the background on the original pop-up page. The story can be contained within one pop-up page, or several pages can be pasted together to make a pop-up book.

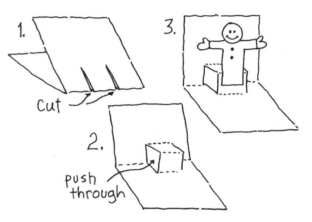

195

WHAT'S THE OPPOSITE?

Play a contradictory challenge game!

OBJECTIVE: Child will use critical-thinking and language skills.

Take turns turning each other's words and statements into the opposite! Start off easy and volunteer words for one another to think of opposites for (hot/cold, rainy/sunny, happy/sad). Then try to turn simple sentences around! For example: A little girl ran home/A big boy walked to the store.

MANY MOVES

Trek, tramp, and traipse to get from here to there!

OBJECTIVE: Child will use creative-thinking and problem-solving skills.

Challenge the child to imagine, describe, and demonstrate as many ways as possible to move from one side of the room to the other! The child can hop, skip, jump, crawl, dance, and move from here to there in a myriad of ways. Add variety by giving the game a new twist. How fast can the child move across the room? How slow? What about how low?

BUTTON SORT

Two-holed, four-holed, skinny, or stout, look at buttons and sort them out!

WHAT YOU'LL NEED: Large buttons, egg carton

OBJECTIVE: Child will sort and classify objects.

Gather together a variety of loose buttons. (Supervise carefully if buttons are small; they could be a choking hazard.) Spread the buttons out and invite the child to sort them. An egg carton can be used for sorting compartments. Encourage the child to choose the sorting categories and then describe them. The child might sort by color, or by number of holes, by size or shape of the buttons, or by pretty and not pretty! If buttons are not available, or for variety, any kind of collection can be used for a sorting activity. The child can sort clean socks from the laundry before they are paired and put away; nuts, bolts, washers, and screws from the hardware drawer; a stack of photographs; etc. To add challenge to the game, after the child has sorted a collection into groups, the child can invent new categories and re-sort the same collection a different way.

198 BACK-TO-BACK PICTURES

Say what you see and then see what you said!

WHAT YOU'LL NEED: Cardboard drawing boards, paper, 2 sets of crayons or markers. Optional: Common household items (rubber bands, paper clips, pennies, etc.)

OBJECTIVE: Child will use speaking, listening, and interpretive skills.

The adult and child can participate in a listen and draw challenge together. Sit back to back, each one holding a drawing board with a piece of paper; a set of crayons or markers should be near each person. One person draws a picture describing step by step what is

being drawn, how it is being drawn, and what colors are being used. The other person draws along, making the same picture based only on the verbal description. When the pictures are finished, turn around and compare the drawings. Then trade roles and try again! For a variation, make copycat pictures. One person draws a simple picture and then the other person (while looking!) draws the same thing. Another variation is to make copycat collages. Gather some household objects (beware of choking hazard). One person arranges a few items on paper to make a simple design. The other person then copies the design.

SOLVE THE PROBLEM 199

Step into a story and solve the problem!

WHAT YOU'LL NEED: Favorite story or book

OBJECTIVE: Child will use problem-solving and creative-thinking skills.

Read a book together, but stop the story at the height of a problem. Then invite the child to describe what he or she might do in a similar situation. Encourage the child to give reasons and explain choices.

BODY PARTS MIX-UP

Mix and match body part pictures to make unusual creatures and critters.

WHAT YOU'LL NEED: Magazine pictures, scissors, paper, nontoxic white glue

OBJECTIVE: Child will develop concept of parts and whole while using creative-thinking skills.

Create an assortment of body part pictures from old magazines. Cut out pictures of people and animals and then cut the pictures further to create an assortment of heads, legs, wings, arms, torsos, and tails. The child can reassemble the body parts to make new creatures and then glue them together on a sheet of paper. The child can then tell about or describe what they have invented, or the child can make up stories about these new creatures!

SINK & FLOAT

Check it out: What will sink and what will float?

WHAT YOU'LL NEED: Tub, water, variety of common items (foam cup, sponge, marble, button, thread spool)

OBJECTIVE: Child will predict, experiment, and draw conclusions.

Gather together an assortment of household items for experimenting (beware of choking hazard if items are small). Everyone should wash their hands before playing in water. Invite the child to explore some of the items in and out of water, enjoying the feel of the water, and observing that some things stay up and some go down to the bottom. After the child has had some exploration time, all the items can be gathered together once more (and new items added), and the child can predict which items will sink and which will float. The child can sort the items into the two categories and then test out the predictions.

SINGING MY OWN SONG

Create new lyrics to old songs!

OBJECTIVE: Child will use listening and creative-thinking skills.

Sing familiar songs with simple melodies, such as "Row, Row, Row, Your Boat" or "Mary Had a Little Lamb." After singing the song, change the words to make up entirely new stories and sing them to the familiar tunes. The new songs can be silly or serious, make-believe or real. To get the child started, invent a new verse about the child and sing it to one of the old familiar tunes. "Mary Had a Little Lamb" can be changed to be a song about the child and a toy or pet that he or she has. Then invite the child to make up the next verse.

FEEL & SORT

Feel and touch, then sort and such!

WHAT YOU'LL NEED: Variety of materials with different textures (sandpaper, bark, erasers, buttons, metal washers, cotton ball, aluminum foil, fabric scraps)

OBJECTIVE: Child will use senses to make comparisons and classify.

Gather together an assortment of items that have different textures. The items should all be large enough so that none can be swallowed. The child can use fingers, hands, and even the face to feel the texture of the items and sort them into simple categories, such as smooth/rough or hard/soft. For more challenge, invite the child to do the sorting with his or her eyes closed and by touch alone, putting smooth things on one side and rough things on the other. For a variation, provide two of each texture. The child can match items by texture with eyes open, or for more challenge with eyes closed!

DIRT COMPARISONS

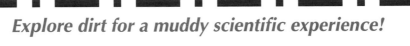

Explore dirt for a muddy scientific experience!

WHAT YOU'LL NEED: 3 cans, spoon, 3 old plates, jar of water

OBJECTIVE: Child will experiment and draw conclusions.

Gather dirt from three different places, and bring the dirt home for comparison. A garden, a vacant lot, and a wooded area have different kinds of dirt. The child can scoop a cupful of

dirt into an empty can or box. To puddle test the three kinds of soil, place each kind of soil on a different plate and form into a shallow volcano shape. The child can add a spoonful of water to each hill of dirt. Then watch what happens to the water and compare the differences. (Sand and potting soil can be puddle-tested too!) To further test each kind of soil, the child can add enough water so that each soil type can be formed into a mud ball. The mud balls can be compared and also observed as they dry. Be sure child washes hands thoroughly when done.

TELL ME THREE REASONS WHY

205

Share personal preferences and back them up with reasons why!

OBJECTIVE: Child will use problem-solving and critical-thinking skills.

Take turns making up preference questions for one another, such as "What do you like better on your pizza, sausage or pepperoni?" "Do you like red or blue better?" "What's more fun, jumping or hopping?" The questioner chooses the question. The person answering reveals a personal preference, but he or she also has to give three reasons why they made that choice!

206

TELL IT TO ME

Illustrate a story and author it too!

WHAT YOU'LL NEED: Paper, markers or crayons, pencil

OBJECTIVE: Child will use language skills to express ideas.

After the child has drawn a picture for a story, invite him or her to dictate the words that tell the story. The words can be written down on the top or bottom of the picture or on a separate piece of paper. Encourage the child's storytelling with questions to elicit story de-

tails such as: What did he do next? Then what happened? Did she have any pets? What did his mother say? How did he feel? When the story is finished, read it back to the child. Ask if the story has been recorded correctly or if there are any other details the child wants to add or change. For more challenge, encourage the child to write the words for his or her story. The child can use invented spelling or lines and scribbles. After the child has "written" the story, have him or her "read" it aloud.

MY HAND IS GRAND

207

Contemplate the marvelous mysteries of just one little hand!

OBJECTIVE: Child will use critical-thinking and problem-solving skills.

Invite the child to think about and list things that can be done with a hand. Record the child's ideas. Give clues to encourage new kinds of thinking. Reread the list together and then keep adding to it. Challenge the child to continue to come up with more ideas! For a variation, challenge the child to demonstrate five different ways to use a hand to make noise, to touch someone, to hold things, etc.

208 EGG CARTON COUNT

Make a more or less comparison counter for intriguing math play.

WHAT YOU'LL NEED: 3 egg cartons, masking tape, tempera paint, brushes, two kinds of counters (paper clips, buttons, acorns, beans)

OBJECTIVE: Child will predict, estimate, compare, and count.

Make a comparison container using three egg cartons. Remove the tops of the cartons and tape the bottoms together to create 2 rows of 18. The child can paint the rows different colors. When the paint has dried, the comparison container can be used to play a predicting game. (Counters should be large enough to avoid a choking hazard or adult should supervise carefully.) Using two different kinds of counters, the child can place a small handful of one kind of counter in one pile and a small handful of the other kind of counter in another pile. Observing the two piles, the child then predicts which pile has the most items and gives a reason for his or her prediction. To check, the child lines up the two different piles of items in the two rows of the comparison container. To make the game more challenging, the child can also predict how many items are in each pile!

A child learns quicker to talk than to be silent.
Norwegian proverb

ARTIST STUDY

Observe an artist's work and work like that artist!

WHAT YOU'LL NEED: Group of children's books illustrated by one artist or book of reproductions of a famous artist's paintings

OBJECTIVE: Child will use observation and interpretative skills.

Gather together several children's books all illustrated by the same artist. After reading the stories, look at the pictures together and talk about the artist's style. Encourage the child to share ideas about that artist's work. What is similar about the pictures in all the books? What colors does the artist like? Are the lines thin or big and bold? Discuss with the child the media the artist uses to make pictures (watercolor, acrylics, chalk, etc.). After making observations about the artist's style, invite the child to make a picture in the same style! The child can make a picture using the same technique.

ART GALLERY TOUR

Create an art gallery and give guided tours!

WHAT YOU'LL NEED: Child's artwork, tape, twine, clothespins

OBJECTIVE: Child will use language skills to express ideas.

Set up an art gallery together by displaying an assortment of the child's artwork. The work can be taped to a wall, clothespinned to a line, or set up on tables and shelves. The child can take family members on a tour of the gallery, describing and telling about each work of art.

WHAT'S IN, OUT, AND IN-BETWEEN?

Create categories, then figure out what fits in and what does not.

 WHAT YOU'LL NEED: Two long lengths of yarn, household objects (paper clips, buttons, washers, crayons, plastic animals, bottle caps, pictures, stuffed animals)

OBJECTIVE: Child will develop math concepts of inclusion and exclusion.

Make two large circles using the two lengths of yarn—have the circles overlap so there is a middle section. This is called a Venn diagram. Explain to the child that you can use the three sections for creating categories. Discuss together the idea of categories and that each circle of yarn will be for a category of items, and the section where the yarn overlaps will be for any items that fit in both categories. Use some of the collected objects as an example (beware of choking hazard with small items). One circle might be for buttons. Place all the buttons from the assorted objects into that circle. The other circle might be for blue things. The child can find all the blue things and place those in the second circle. That might include a blue crayon, a blue plastic animal, and a blue bottle cap. Ask the child if there are any

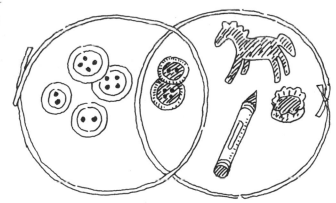

items that are both buttons and blue? Explain that those items fit in both categories, so they go in the middle section. Remove all the items from the two circles and intersecting section and place them back in the group of assorted items. Invite the child to come up with two new categories for the items and to create a new Venn diagram. Pictures can also be used to sort into the two circles.

WHAT IF?

212

Imagine and invent right along with the story.

OBJECTIVE: Child will use creative-thinking skills.

Share simple stories and use them as springboards for creative thinking. Engage the child in discussion throughout the storytelling, stopping along the way to invite the child to share ideas. Ask questions like: What might happen if . . . ? What do you think will happen next? What makes you think that? What would you do if you were in the story? How do you think the grandfather feels? What else could he do? What else could the little girl have done? What would have happened if the dog stayed outside? Can you think of another way the story could have ended?

213

NUMBER RIDDLES

Invent and tell number riddles!

OBJECTIVE: Child will use critical-thinking and problem-solving skills.

Share some simple number riddles with the child such as: What has four legs but never walks anywhere? (A chair.) What is a calf after it is six months old? (Seven months old.) How many legs does a dog have if you call its tail a leg? (Four—calling a tail a leg doesn't make it one.) A girl was four on her last birthday and will be six on her next birthday—how is this possible? (Today is her fifth birthday!) How do you divide five potatoes evenly between three people? (You mash them.) Why is the longest nose only 11 inches long? (Because if it were 12 inches it would be a foot.) After sharing and talking about several riddles, challenge the child to invent new ones! Be prepared for the riddles to be very silly and for them to make very little sense at first.

STORY SWITCHEROO

214

Tell a story in a mixed-up way!

OBJECTIVE: Child will use problem-solving and sequencing skills.

The adult makes simple drawings to represent the four main events of a favorite story or well-known fairytale. Draw each picture on a separate piece of paper. Lay out the pictures in order and retell the story using the pictures as prompts. After you have finished telling the story in the traditional way, turn over the pictures and have the child mix them up. The child can then turn them over in the mixed-up order and reinvent the story, telling it using the new sequence. For more of a challenge, the child can draw the pictures for the activity.

215

WHAT'S THE MOOD?

Share, discuss, and sort happy and sad pictures.

WHAT YOU'LL NEED: Magazine pictures, labeled sorting boxes

OBJECTIVE: Child will use critical-thinking and interpretative skills to sort and classify.

Gather an assortment of pictures of people and animals cut from magazines. Label two boxes, one with a happy face and one with a sad face. Invite the child to sort the pictures into the happy and sad boxes. Encourage the child to tell about the choices made. Later on, add other categories, such as angry and frightened. The child might want to suggest categories as well, such as excited or sleepy.

TUNNEL HOLE ROLL

216

Make a bending, turning, long marble tunnel roll!

WHAT YOU'LL NEED: Cardboard tubes, scissors, masking tape, marbles, blocks

OBJECTIVE: Child will predict, experiment, and draw conclusions.

Be sure this activity is supervised—marbles are choking hazards! Make the tunnel tube with the child by using cardboard tubes from wrapping paper, paper towels, and toilet paper. Make slits in the end of one tube and then slip another tube inside the first. The tubes can be angled and then taped together. Five, six, seven, or more tubes can be attached to make long winding tunnels. The child can then set one end on a block or chair and roll a marble through. The child can experiment by placing the tube at higher or lower levels and also reangling the bends. Invite the child to share findings and conclusions after experimenting.

217

WHAT HAPPENED LAST?

For fun and challenge, retell a story from the end to the beginning!

OBJECTIVE: Child will use critical-thinking and problem-solving skills.

Invite the child to retell a favorite story, but to tell it backward, starting with the end first! The child tells the ending, then what happened just before that, and then just before that. Prompt the child with questions that help guide the storytelling back to the start . . . which is the end! To simplify the backward retelling, ask the child to tell the ending, two things that happen in the middle, and then the beginning.

DRY & SPY

218

Investigate evaporation!

WHAT YOU'LL NEED: Variety of household materials (cotton ball, paper towel, sponge, fabric swatches, piece of cardboard), twine, clothespins, bowl, water. Optional: Paper, pencil

OBJECTIVE: Child will predict, experiment, and draw conclusions.

Gather together a variety of materials for testing, and set up a twine drying line. The child can soak each of the materials in a bowl of water and then clip each to the line with a clothespin. The child can make predictions about which things will dry first, last, and how long they will each take. The child can also test the drying time for the same item inside and outside—do the objects take the same time to dry inside and out? If not, which dries first, the outside item or the inside one? Are the results the same on a windy day as on a day with no wind? On a sunny day and a cloudy day? The child can observe the results and make conclusions about discoveries. For a greater challenge, the child can also chart the results.

219

WRAPPING PAPER STORIES

*Create wordless books from wrapping paper,
and read the books!*

WHAT YOU'LL NEED: Construction paper, stapler, wrapping paper with large patterns, scissors, nontoxic white glue

OBJECTIVE: Child will use creative-thinking and language skills.

Make a blank booklet by folding several sheets of paper in half and stapling them along the fold. Then invite the child to make a wordless book by cutting pictures out of the wrapping paper and gluing them into the book. When the book is finished, the child can make up a story and "read" the book by telling a story to go with the pictures.

220 WHAT CAN SHAPES MAKE?

Turn triangles, circles, squares, and rectangles into houses, horses, or bears!

WHAT YOU'LL NEED: Construction paper shapes (circles, squares, triangles, rectangles) cut in different sizes and colors, paper, nontoxic white glue, crayons or markers

OBJECTIVE: Child will gain experience with shapes while using problem-solving and creative-thinking skills.

Provide the child with a piece of paper, glue, and an assortment of construction paper circles, squares, triangles, and rectangles cut in different colors and sizes. The child can choose shapes and arrange and glue them to make pictures—creating animals, people, vehicles, trees, houses, and assorted other things from the shapes. Give the child crayons or markers to add extra details to the picture. For a variation, make stencils of small, medium, and large circles, squares, rectangles, and triangles for the child to explore and draw with, or cut cardboard shapes for the child to trace!

The purpose of education is to awaken joy in creative expression and knowledge.
Albert Einstein

ONE WORD DRAMA

Take a word and act it out!

OBJECTIVE: Child will use creative-thinking and problem-solving skills.

Take turns making up actions to dramatize single words. Start with simple action words, such as hop, wiggle, laugh. Feeling words can also be part of the game (happy, sad, sleepy, grumpy, excited). Choose words to act out for the others to guess! Other variations include using position words (inside, around, under, through) and action words (sleep, read, eat, cook, drive).

MORNING, AFTERNOON & EVENING

Make a times-of-the-day collage.

WHAT YOU'LL NEED: Construction paper, nontoxic white glue, scissors, old magazines

OBJECTIVE: Child will classify and sequence.

The child can create a sequence collage to show the different kinds of activities that happen at different times of the day. Tape three different colored pieces of construction paper together to make a long piece of paper with three sections. Explain to the child that the first section of the collage is for pictures that show things people do in the morning when a day begins. The middle paper is for activities people do in the middle of the day. And the last section of the paper is for things that happen at the end of the day. Ask the child to tell you about different kinds of things he or she does in the morning, in the middle of the day, or during the evening when the day is ending. Then invite the child to find pictures in magazines to cut out that illustrate morning, afternoon, and evening activities.

223

BOX TOWN

▼▼▼▼▼▼▼▼▼▼▼▼▼▼▼▼▼▼▼▼▼▼▼▼▼▼▼▼▼▼▼▼

Build a box town!

 WHAT YOU'LL NEED: Wide assortment of boxes (including empty food boxes and washed milk cartons), newspaper, masking tape, nontoxic white glue, paint, brushes

OBJECTIVE: Child will use creative-thinking and problem-solving skills.

The child can use an assortment of boxes in different shapes and sizes to make the town. Spread newspaper on the ground where the town will be set up. The buildings can be made of separate boxes or from several boxes glued together. The finished buildings can be painted. Milk cartons can be painted successfully if a little glue is added to the paint. Streets and parks can be painted onto the newspaper. When the town is finished, the child can then name and describe the town. For more challenge, the child can make a map of the box town showing each of the buildings and any streets or parks.

YES OR NO?

● ●

224

Play a cooperative "Could it be?" guessing game.

OBJECTIVE: Child will use problem-solving, critical-thinking, and language skills.

Take turns making up true or silly statements to report to each other. One person makes a factual or funny statement, such as "I'm wearing blue shoes," "There's a giraffe in our backyard," "Uncle Pete loves baseball," or "We're going to have baked hats for dinner." Then the listener thinks about whether such a thing could be true and answers yes or no. For more challenge, encourage the child to give reasons for each yes and no answer.

HEY! A SURVEY!

Take a tally of friends, neighbors, and family.

WHAT YOU'LL NEED: Paper, pencil, clipboard or cardboard and large paper clip, string or yarn

OBJECTIVE: Child will use graphing skills to record and interpret data.

The child can survey family members, friends, and neighbors on a topic of choices and record results on a simple tally sheet. For simple tallies, the survey can either be in the form of a yes/no question (Do you like chocolate ice cream?) or a simple two-choice question (What do you like better, dogs or cats?). The child can make up the question. Create a check-off tally sheet with two rows, one labeled "Yes" and the other labeled "No," or with two other choices. The tally sheet can be clipped on a clipboard or to a piece of cardboard with a paper clip. Tie the pencil onto the clipboard with yarn so the child won't be walking around holding the pencil. The child can survey friends and family, record the result, and then use the chart to report on the outcome. For more challenge, help the child come up with a commu-

nity issue question for a neighborhood survey, such as "Do you think we need a stop sign at the corner?" or "Do you think dogs should always be on leashes?" Create a tally form and accompany the child to survey the neighbors!

COLOR SORT

Mix and match and sort a varied array of colored chips.

WHAT YOU'LL NEED: Paint chips (free at paint or hardware store), scissors, clear contact paper

OBJECTIVE: Child will sort and classify.

You and the child can cut the paint chips into color squares. The child can sort the chips into color groups by choosing categories. He or she can then record choices or make a design by placing chips on the sticky side of a piece of clear contact paper. Place a second sheet of clear contact paper on top to seal the color record. For more challenge, the child can place the color chips in order, explaining the reason for the choice of ordering.

MOOD DANCE

Make up mood movements for happy, sad, and mad dances!

227

OBJECTIVE: Child will use creative-thinking skills.

Invite the child to create different dances to express different kinds of moods. The child can choose one mood and make up a dance. Encourage the child to imagine and invent hand movements, footsteps, and whole body jumps, skips, and hops that show the mood chosen. The child can also think about tempo and rhythm to express the mood. For a variation, play a mood dance guessing game. Take turns making up and demonstrating happy, sad, frightened, or mad dances. One person performs a mood dance and the other person guesses the mood.

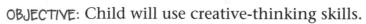

CUP PUPPETS

Make pop-up puppets for peek-a-boo stories!

 WHAT YOU'LL NEED: Polystyrene cup, 2 to 3 unsharpened pencils, stiff paper, nontoxic white glue, crayons or markers

OBJECTIVE: Child will use creative-thinking and language skills.

The child can make the puppets by drawing characters on stiff paper and cutting them out. Glue the characters to the eraser ends of the pencils. The adult can then pierce a hole in the bottom of the cup, and the child can insert the blunt ends of the pencil puppets. The child holds the puppet under the cup. A puppet is pushed out of the cup to come onstage and is slipped back into the cup to go offstage. One cup can be the stage for up to three puppets.

BEASTLY BABBLE

Tell the tales the animals might say!

 WHAT YOU'LL NEED: Magazine pictures, construction paper, nontoxic white glue, crayons or markers

OBJECTIVE: Child will use creative-thinking skills.

Use animal pictures as a spark for creative interpretation and tale-telling. Cut out pictures of a variety of animals from magazines and paste them onto a piece of construction paper. Share the pictures, and encourage the child to consider what the animals in the pictures might say if they could talk. The pictures can be labeled with the child's ideas and then later bound into a book, if desired.

SHINY PENNIES

230

Experiment and explore penny polishing!

WHAT YOU'LL NEED: 3 plastic cups, vinegar, salt, lemon juice, soapy water, cotton swabs, pennies, paper towels

OBJECTIVE: Child will predict, experiment, and draw conclusions.

Prepare three solutions: vinegar and salt, lemon juice, and soapy water. The child can predict, test, and tell which solution will clean the pennies best. The child can dip the pennies in the solutions and then scrub them with cotton swabs. Let them dry on paper towels. After testing, invite the child to share ideas on why one solution works the best. Explain that the vinegar and salt caused a chemical reaction that dissolves the copper oxide that darkens the penny. The child can experiment further by testing to see if the vinegar and salt solution will clean other things. Other kinds of coins can be tested, as well as other materials.

231

PROP PROMPTING

Use story props for friendly hint helpers in storytelling.

WHAT YOU'LL NEED: Props related to stories

OBJECTIVE: Child will use creative-thinking and language skills.

After sharing a favorite story, fairy tale, or nursery rhyme, provide the child with some simple props that relate to the story or rhyme. Place the book along with the props in a place where the child is free to dramatize and act! The child can use the props as prompters for retelling and acting out the story or rhyme.

232 WATCHING BEANS GROW

Plant a bean, and watch and record its growth.

WHAT YOU'LL NEED: Lima bean, soil, jar or can, watering can, paper, crayons, yarn, scissors, nontoxic white glue. Optional: Craft stick

OBJECTIVE: Child will use observation and sequencing skills.

The child can plant a bean in a can or jar, set it in a sunny place, water it, and make sure the soil stays moist. A lima bean grows very quickly. The child can record the growth in drawings, making a picture each day of what the plant looks like. At a later time, the pictures can be mixed up and the child can lay them out and put them back in order according to the growth pictured. The child can also record the growth of the plant by measuring it. Starting when the bean plant appears above the surface of the dirt, the child can measure the plant with a piece of yarn. Each day the child can cut a piece of yarn the same height as the plant. The

lengths of yarn can be glued on paper in a row next to one another, charting the growth of the plant. For more challenge, a craft stick that has inches or centimeters marked off on it can be inserted in the soil. The child can note how tall the plant is each day and color in squares on a graph to represent the height and graph the growth.

Education is light, lack of it is darkness.
Russian proverb

WHAT'S ALL AROUND ME— OBSERVING & LISTENING!

Young children construct knowledge through active learning and hands-on discovery. They are eager and enthusiastic to perform nonstop serious life research and find out everything they can about all that is around them. Observing and listening are essential to the process. As children observe, listen, and notice all that is around them, they form assumptions about their world. They begin to wonder and question. They want to explore. They experiment to test their assumptions and find answers to their questions. And then they observe and notice once more in order to refine the ever-growing understanding of the world they are constructing. This chapter contains activities that enrich and support observing and listening.

233 HEAR THE BEAT

Listen for the beat in the sounds of a day!

OBJECTIVE: Child will use listening and observation skills.

The child can listen to music and try to find the beat—then he or she can clap to it or tap to it to get familiar with it. Then, to take the activity further, the child can listen for beats going on around him or her naturally—the sounds of people walking on a sidewalk, a construction worker hammering, the clothes in a dryer thumping. Encourage the child to listen for those beats and try to tap and clap to them also!

SPRIGS AND TWIGS

234

Start a twig collection.

WHAT YOU'LL NEED: Paper bag

OBJECTIVE: Child will sort and classify.

The child can search on the ground and around different kinds of trees to gather twigs. The child can place the twigs in the bag, which the adult should carry. When the child is finished, carry the twigs home. The child can then sort and classify the twigs according to their different attributes. For more advanced study, check out a book from the library that has pictures or diagrams of twigs from different trees. Each kind of tree has twigs that have specific characteristics. The child can begin to learn to recognize some of the characteristics of twigs from several of the trees.

SECRET SIGHTS

235

Play a camouflage game.

WHAT YOU'LL NEED: Three or four common household items, tape

OBJECTIVE: Child will use observation and problem-solving skills.

Take turns hiding items in the open for the other person to find. Choose several common items, such as a wooden spoon, a small box, a bar of soap, or a polystyrene grocery tray. Both adult and child note and agree on the items to be used for the game. Then one person leaves the room and the other hides all the items, but in places where they can be seen if looked for carefully. The items are hidden in full view, not under beds or inside boxes. A wooden spoon might be taped to the side of a wooden cupboard so the colors make it hard to spot. It is hidden in sight—not out of sight! After all the items are hidden, the other person tries to find them. Then choose new items and play again.

SEEDS I SEE

236

Search for seeds in everyday foods!

 WHAT YOU'LL NEED: Stiff paper, nontoxic white glue, markers or crayons

OBJECTIVE: Child will use observation skills.

The child can save the seeds found in fresh fruits and vegetables and start a collection. Let the child wash and dry the seeds, then glue them onto stiff paper to make a chart. The child can draw a picture next to each glued seed of the food in which the seed was found. To make a seed matching game, the child can glue one of each kind of seed to small squares of stiff paper. A picture of the food is drawn on the back of the paper for self-checking. A second picture of the food is drawn on another paper square. The child can match the seed cards to the picture cards, turning over the seed cards to check the matches.

237

NATURE COLLAGE

Collect and compare and collage!

WHAT YOU'LL NEED: Bag, nature items (twigs, bark, leaves, petals, seeds, pine needles, pebbles, even a little dirt), egg carton, cardboard, nontoxic white glue

OBJECTIVE: Child will observe and compare.

The child can collect nature items in a bag, and then bring them home to look at more carefully and compare. The child might want to use an egg carton to sort some of the findings. After observing and examining all the assorted items, the child can arrange and glue some of them onto cardboard to create a nature collage. For easier gluing, have the child put glue on the cardboard first, then place the items on the glue.

238

IT SOUNDS LIKE THIS!

▼▼▼▼▼▼▼▼▼▼▼▼▼▼▼▼▼▼▼▼▼▼▼▼▼▼▼▼▼▼▼▼▼

Use imagination and skill to imitate natural sounds!

OBJECTIVE: Child will use critical-thinking and listening skills.

Challenge the child to listen to the sounds all around and to invent sounds to imitate them. The child might try to imitate natural sounds, such as wind, rain, or thunder, or household sounds, such as running water or the broom when a parent sweeps the floor. For more challenge, play a sound guessing game by imitating nature and household sounds for one another to guess.

NATURE WALK

239

Take a woody walk and predict what the sights might be.

WHAT YOU'LL NEED: Marker, pad of paper, pencil

OBJECTIVE: Child will predict and observe.

Plan a walk in the woods or through a park. Talk together first about what different things might be seen or heard. Make a picture list of all the predictions to take along. The

list might include birds, squirrels, flowers, trees, rocks, ants, and people. The child can check off items along the way. When you return to the house, check the list together to see how many of the predicted items were seen and also to note and add important observations that were not predicted beforehand! For a variation, take a walk and ask the child to predict how many of one kind of thing might be seen, such as how many birds sitting in trees, red flowers, dogs on leashes, and then count them together.

240 · CIRCLE SEARCH

Hunt through the house in search of circles!

OBJECTIVE: Child will learn shape recognition and use observation skills.

The child can go on a circle hunt looking for things that are circles and gathering circle objects. The child might note a circle window, the circle of a lamp shade, a globe, or the almost circle of a toilet bowl! Objects the child can gather might include a penny, paper plate, washer, button, jar top, or a marble (watch carefully for choking hazards). Variations include scouting for squares and traversing for triangles!

241 — ROCK & ROLL

Make, shake, and compare noises!

WHAT YOU'LL NEED: Empty coffee cans and lids, assortment of common objects (rock, button, cork, cotton ball, bottle cap, paper clip, magnet, eraser)

OBJECTIVE: Child will use listening skills to observe and compare.

Gather several cans and an assortment of objects to use for noisemakers. Invite the child to examine the objects and guess which would make the loudest or softest shaker noises. The child can then test out guesses, placing one object in a can at a time and comparing the noises different objects make. Two cans with an object in each (or three objects in three cans) can be compared at a time. If more cans are available, after initial comparisons, the child can place every object into an individual can and try to identify the content of each can by the noise each makes. (Small objects may pose a choking hazard!)

LEAF AND FLOWER PRESSING

242

Press and preserve flowers and leaves for pictures and for saving.

WHAT YOU'LL NEED: Leaves, flowers, paper towels, newspapers, telephone books or heavy books. Optional: Paper, nontoxic white glue, clear contact paper

OBJECTIVE: Child will observe and experiment.

The child can collect leaves and flowers for pressing. Let the child place the leaves and flowers between two sheets of paper towel. The child can place this paper towel-flower sandwich on top of a stack of newspaper, and then place more folded newspaper on top. Place heavy books or telephone books on top of the newspapers. The flowers or leaves will take about three to four weeks to dry out and flatten. The child can peek and check the progress regularly during that time. After the flowers have flattened and dried, the child can use them to make a collage, seal them between two sheets of clear contact paper, or save them in a box or in a book!

243

NIGHT SCENES

Depict the deep of night with dark paper pictures.

WHAT YOU'LL NEED: Black construction paper, pastels or colored chalk. Optional: Sticker stars

OBJECTIVE: Child will record personal experiences and observations.

Invite the child to draw nighttime (inside or outside) pictures using dark paper to inspire nighttime thinking. Chalk and pastels both show up brightly on black paper, adding sparkle to working on a project about the dark. For a variation, add sticker stars to the materials.

IT'S FOR THE BIRDS!

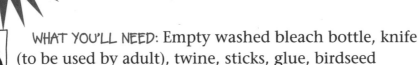

Make a bird feeder and watch the birds!

WHAT YOU'LL NEED: Empty washed bleach bottle, knife (to be used by adult), twine, sticks, glue, birdseed

OBJECTIVE: Child will use observation skills.

Cut holes in an empty washed bleach bottle. Cut two small holes at the top for twine to hang the bird feeder, one big hole in the middle for the bird to slip in and out of, and several small holes around the bottom to insert twigs for perches. The child can find and collect the perch sticks, fit them into the holes, and glue them to make them secure. Fill the bottom of the container with birdseed, and hang the feeder in a tree. The child can watch the bird feeder and report on observations. (Parents and child should clean out the feeder periodically to keep birds from getting sick.) For more challenge, the child can keep track of sightings, noting how many birds are seen at the feeder at different times during the day, or at the same time on different days.

I DID SPY

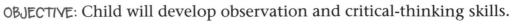

Play a variation of the traditional "I Spy" game.

OBJECTIVE: Child will develop observation and critical-thinking skills.

This game can be played indoors or out. Taking turns, one person starts by taking a look all around and then closing his or her eyes. The second person, with eyes open, asks questions for the first person to answer with eyes closed. The questions are quick-take observation questions, such as: Is your blue sweater on the bed or the chair? How many books are on the table? What color is the towel on the line?

246 DO BIRDS MAKE BIRDS' NESTS BEST?

Take a bird-nest test, and try to build a better bird nest!

WHAT YOU'LL NEED: Twigs, leaves, yarn, cotton, feathers, string, grass, weeds, dirt, water. Optional: Modeling clay

OBJECTIVE: Child will experiment, observe, and draw conclusions.

Gather together common items that birds use to build nests. Challenge the child to use the same materials and attempt to create a bird's nest. The child can mold the items and try gluing them together using mud! The child might also enjoy making a bird out of modeling clay to sit in the handmade bird's nest!

LETTER COLLAGE 247

Create a colorful letter montage using letters cut from magazines.

WHAT YOU'LL NEED: Construction paper, old magazines, scissors, nontoxic white glue

OBJECTIVE: Child will develop letter recognition.

The adult and child can search through magazines and newspapers and cut out letters (the adult may need to do the cutting). Have the child glue the letters onto construction paper to make a collage design. As a variation, the child can make a number collage. The child can also search for the letters in his or her name and make a name picture.

248 SEEDS ON THE UP-AND-UP!

Perform an experiment to see if seeds know which way is up!

WHAT YOU'LL NEED: 4 lima beans, clear plastic jar or cup, potting soil, black construction paper, tape, plastic wrap, rubber band

OBJECTIVE: Child will experiment, observe, and draw conclusions.

The child can fill the jar with potting soil and push a seed into the soil right next to the edge of the jar where it can be seen. The other three seeds are also pushed in around the jar. The child can moisten the soil and check it daily (keeping it moist) until the seeds begin to sprout. Once the seeds have sprouted, wrap and tape the black paper around the jar. Make a greenhouse lid with plastic wrap and a rubber band. This will keep moisture in and prevent soil from spilling. Have the child place the jar on its side for three days; then turn it upside down for three days. For the next three days, place it on its side again; for the final three days set it right side up. (Keep checking the moisture level throughout the process, and add water when needed.) After the 12 days of rotation, the black paper is removed and the child can note that the beans kept changing their growth pattern so they were always heading up. Encourage the child to draw conclusions about the reason for this. The adult and child can also keep track of what they have done by drawing pictures of how they placed the jar. The adult can letter each picture with dates of when the jar was placed in that position.

HUNTING FOR SOUNDS

249

Seek sounds that are all around to catch and collect!

WHAT YOU'LL NEED: Tape recorder, blank tape. Optional: Paper, crayons or markers

OBJECTIVE: Child will use critical-thinking and listening skills.

Go on a sound search, taking a walk outside or a listening walk through the house. Invite the child to listen to all the sounds around and to choose several to collect. The sounds can be collected by imitating and repeating them or by recording them. After the sound search is over, the child can share the saved sounds by repeating the remembered ones or playing the tape and telling about what made the sounds that were recorded. The child can also draw pictures of the people, animals, or things that made the sounds that were collected!

SILHOUETTE SPRAY

250

Paint around to see the shape!

WHAT YOU'LL NEED: Plastic spray bottles, thinned tempera paint, construction paper, tape, nature items (leaves, twigs, rocks, flowers, etc.)

OBJECTIVE: Child will use observation skills as part of creative exploration.

Create a nature painting of silhouette shapes. The child can collect nature items and then tape them to construction paper. The child may choose to tape one item on each piece of paper or may prefer to make a nature medley, taping several items on a large paper. After the items are taped in place, the child can spray the entire paper with paint using the spray bottle filled with thinned tempera paint. When the paint is dry, the child can remove the items to reveal their silhouette shapes.

251

KEEPING TRACK OF A TREE

Adopt a tree to visit and observe.

WHAT YOU'LL NEED: Paper, crayons, pencil. Optional: Disposable camera

OBJECTIVE: Child will observe and record changes, and use language and emergent-writing skills.

The child can choose a nearby tree to visit and watch for a long period of time—a season or even a year. The child can visit the tree weekly or biweekly. On each visit the child can draw a picture of it and note changes in appearance, dictating observations to an adult or writing in a journal. The child can also use a disposable camera to document the changes over the year.

252

SAME AS ME

Make measuring meaningful by measuring with me!

WHAT YOU'LL NEED: Yarn, scissors

OBJECTIVE: Child will measure and compare.

The child can use his or her own height as the unit of measure! Measure the child with yarn and cut a piece the same length as the child's height. Then challenge the child to use the yarn to find something the same height as the yarn length, something shorter than the yarn length, and something taller than the yarn length. The activity can be done both indoors and out. For a variation, cut yarn the length of the child's foot, arm, or hand for the child to measure with.

SKY DANCING

253

Choreograph the heavens!

OBJECTIVE: Child will use critical, interpretive, and creative-thinking skills.

Invite the child to think about and imagine how the sky moves and what a sky dance might look like. Encourage the child to ponder questions such as: How does the wind move? How would rain dance? Do clouds have rhythm? The child can listen to music and invent sky dances that interpret different kinds of weather through movement.

254

VEHICLE TALLY

Keep track of cars and trucks with a graph and tally!

WHAT YOU'LL NEED: Clipboard or piece of cardboard, tally sheet divided into 3 to 5 columns labeled with simple pictures of common vehicles (car, police car, fire engine, truck, bus), pencil

OBJECTIVE: Child will sort, count, and graph.

Make the tally sheet. Then go to a park or your frontyard, somewhere it is easy to sit and watch cars driving by. Invite the child to predict what kind of vehicle will pass by most often. Label each of the columns (pictures are best). The child can choose the column categories. The child might choose vehicle types (truck, car, motorcycle, van) or car colors (yellow cars, blue cars, red cars). Write down predictions of what the child expects to see the most and least of. Then let the child keep track of the sightings by tallying the passing cars in the correct columns. When one of the columns is all checked off, stop the tally and check against the predictions. For a further challenge, take the same tally at different times of the day or on different days, and compare all the tallies to see if the results are the same or different.

WATER VIEWER

255

Make a water viewer and view what's under water!

WHAT YOU'LL NEED: Milk carton, heavy clear plastic wrap, rubber band

OBJECTIVE: Child will experiment and observe.

Cut the top and bottom off an empty washed milk carton. Help the child

place heavy clear plastic wrap over one end and secure it in place with a rubber band. The child can submerge this end in a pond and look through the open end to view underwater happenings more easily. (Adults should always supervise children around water!) If there is no pond nearby, the child can use the water viewer in a bathtub or wading pool, placing small toys or pebbles underwater to be viewed.

256

WAX PAPER WINDOW

Turn a pretty collage into a see-through window.

WHAT YOU'LL NEED: Wax paper, leaves, flat nature items, iron.
Optional: Ribbons, yarn, crayon scrapings

OBJECTIVE: Child will observe, compare, and use creative-thinking skills.

The child can collect flat nature items and arrange them on wax paper. Ribbons, yarn, or crayon scrapings can also be added for extra decoration. When the child has finished assembling the design, the adult can iron a second sheet of wax paper on top to create a sealed nature window.

257

HARK! I SEE BARK!

Record and remember trees with bark rubbings!

WHAT YOU'LL NEED: Thin paper, crayons

OBJECTIVE: Child will observe and compare.

Peel the paper off several crayons and go out bark hunting! The child can choose the trees to record and the crayon color to record them with. Hold the paper against the tree as the child makes the rubbing. The child can make rubbings on different kinds of trees and compare the different impressions they make. As a variation, the child can make building rubbings, making impressions of different materials (stone, wood, stucco, cement) and comparing them.

SEED FARMING

258

Cultivate seeds to eat!

WHAT YOU'LL NEED: Seeds for sprouting (alfalfa, mung, radish), jar, cheesecloth, rubber band, water

OBJECTIVE: Child will explore and observe natural changes.

Sprout seeds for a lunch salad or sandwich or to steam for a dinner vegetable. The child can measure a spoonful of seeds into a jar and then fill the jar with lukewarm water. The seeds should sit overnight in the water. In the morning, place a piece of cheesecloth over the top of the jar and secure it with the rubber band. The child can then pour out the water, while the seeds stay secure in the jar. The child can then fill the jar with fresh water, jiggle the jar to rinse the seeds, and pour out the fresh water. Then have the child refill the jar with water. The seeds should be rinsed several times a day. In a day or two the seeds will begin to sprout. Within a few days, the seeds will have sprouted and be ready to eat!

PLANT PARTS SALAD

259

Make a root, stem, leaf, flower, and seed salad!

WHAT YOU'LL NEED: Salad ingredients, bowl, salad servers, plates, salad forks

OBJECTIVE: Child will use critical-thinking and observation skills.

Go shopping together for the ingredients for the plant parts salad. Explain to the child that you will need one of each kind of plant part for the salad. The child can make the choices! At the market, point out several items in each category (one category at a time). The child can choose a root part from among carrots, radishes, or parsnips; a stem from celery or leeks; leaves from spinach or lettuce; flowers from cauliflower or broccoli; and seeds from sunflower or sprouted alfalfa. Purchase the ingredients and come home and make the plant parts salad together! For a variation, make a tree salad, using only things that grow on trees as ingredients!

260

WHAT I SAW

Tell all about what happened without words!

OBJECTIVE: Child will use observation, communication, and creative-expression skills.

Invite the child to tell about something he or she did—but do it without talking. The child can report all about an afternoon adventure, visit, or walk, and all that happened and was observed—but tell the tale without words! Challenge the child to report observations through pantomime. To simplify, allow the child to use one word clues to help communicate each pantomime action.

261 SEED TASTE TEST

Take a seed taste test and tell which seeds taste best!

WHAT YOU'LL NEED: Variety of edible seeds (sunflower, peanuts, sprouts, popped corn, coconut), small paper plates, magnifying glass

OBJECTIVE: Child will experiment and make comparisons.

Wash hands first! Gather together a variety of seeds that can be eaten as food. Invite the child to observe and compare the seeds. The child can use the magnifying glass for careful observation, noting differences in size, shape, and color. Then the child can eat the seeds and note the differences in taste! Discuss with the child which seeds they like best and which seeds they like least.

SNOW CREAM 262

Make a cool treat to eat with freshly fallen snow!

WHAT YOU'LL NEED: Fresh clean snow, confectioners' sugar, vanilla extract, cream, spoon, bowl. Optional: Food coloring, magnifying glass

OBJECTIVE: Child will use observation and language skills.

Have everyone wash their hands first! The child can make a snow cream treat by mixing fresh (clean!) snow in a bowl with a spoonful of sugar, a drop of vanilla, and a little cream. Add a few drops of food coloring to give the snow some color! Then let the child eat and describe. (Be sure to use fresh snow immediately after or even during a snowfall.) For more challenge, have the child observe snowflakes under a magnifying glass!

263 STILL-LIFE PAINTINGS

Look carefully and paint what you see!

 WHAT YOU'LL NEED: Paper, paint, brushes, flowers or potted plant

OBJECTIVE: Child will develop observation skills in order to record details.

 Invite the child to paint a picture of a potted plant, a vase of flowers, or other natural items that the child can look at and study while painting. Assemble the still life with the child. Share picture books with paintings of still lifes by artists whose styles are very different. Help the child understand that all the artists started by looking at the things they painted, but that they all had a different way of seeing. Encourage the child to look closely at the still life you've created together and to paint it as he or she sees it.

PRETEND HIKE 264

Create a picnic path inside and follow the trail!

 WHAT YOU'LL NEED: Pillows, newspaper, picnic lunch, backpack

OBJECTIVE: Child will use creative and interpretive thinking.

The child can create a pretend mountain path in the home. Turn pillows into hills to climb up, a chair into a large tree to walk around, newspapers into a stream to jump over—we don't want wet feet! The child can map out the mountain path, then pack a lunch to carry in a backpack on the trek. The child can follow the path to a designated mountaintop and then eat the picnic lunch or snack there.

265

THE LOCAL SCENE

Create a mural of the neighborhood highlights.

WHAT YOU'LL NEED: Large paper, crayons, markers. Optional: Disposable camera

OBJECTIVE: Child will use critical-thinking and observation skills.

After taking a research tour of the neighborhood, the child can try to recall as many details as possible and draw them on a large paper. The adult and child can then take another walk through the neighborhood to see if there are any important buildings, trees, houses, or other street details that the child wants to add. For more challenge, the child can make a mural or a map of the area, drawing the location of the buildings, roads, and sidewalks in the neighborhood. The child can also use a camera to record scenes of the neighborhood. The child can use the pictures when drawing the mural, as a reference for map making, or as a separate activity, for sequencing. To sequence the pictures, the child can line them up in the same order as the buildings on the block.

266

OPPOSITES OBSERVATION

Go ogling for opposites all around!

OBJECTIVE: Child will develop concept and recognition of opposites, and use observation and problem-solving skills.

This search can take place outside or inside. The child looks for two things that display opposite attributes, such as something fast and something slow; something quiet and something loud; something big and something little. Encourage the child to come up with new categories of opposites! For a variation, together look at magazines or picture books and find opposites in the pictures.

COLORS AROUND ME

267

Go color sleuthing up and down, all around town!

WHAT YOU'LL NEED: 8 to 10 white index cards, crayons

OBJECTIVE: Child will use observation and problem-solving skills.

Have the child color a different color on each card. Invite the child to choose one card for some neighborhood detective work. Then take a walk around the block, bringing the color card along to match colors. The child can carry the card and search for houses, cars, signs, flowers, and other things that are the same color as on the card. For a variation, go shape, number, or letter searching. For each kind of search, help the child prepare the cards to carry along to help focus the detective work.

268

CREEPY CRAWLY EXPLORATION

Explore the earth up close and personal!

WHAT YOU'LL NEED: Magnifying glass

OBJECTIVE: Child will use critical-thinking and observation skills.

Find a grassy area where the child can stretch out on the ground. Invite the child to choose one little attractive patch of earth and spend some time closely observing what goes on there! The child can use the magnifying glass and note what is there and what is happening. Encourage the child to describe the earthy discoveries by asking open-ended questions, such as: What seems to be moving? How does it seem to move? What color is it?

269

WHAT'S INSIDE?

Predict what's inside fruits and vegetables!

WHAT YOU'LL NEED: Variety of fruits or vegetables with seeds (avocado, lemon, apple, pumpkin), knife (for adult use only), small paper cups

OBJECTIVE: Child will predict, estimate, and count.

Invite the child to look at different fruits or vegetables and predict how many seeds are inside. Then cut open the fruit or vegetable and take a look. Encourage the child to make an estimate after viewing the seeds before counting them. Then count to check! The child can count the seeds for foods with single or only a few seeds. The adult and child can count higher numbers together. For foods with lots and lots and lots of seeds (pumpkins), use paper cups to count by tens. Plant some of the seeds after counting. The avocado seed will sprout if you pierce it with three or four toothpicks and place it in a jar of water with the pointy side up. Refrigerate apple seeds for six weeks in a moist paper towel before planting so they think winter has just ended. Instead of planting the pumpkin seeds, toast them and enjoy them as a treat!

All our knowledge has its origins in our perceptions.
Leonardo da Vinci

FLOWER BEADS

270

Make scented beads from fragrant flowers.

WHAT YOU'LL NEED: 3 cups fragrant petals (such as rose petals), scissors, large spoon, bowl, ⅓ cup flour, 1 tablespoon salt, 2 teaspoons water, pencil, wire cooling rack, darning needle, yarn

OBJECTIVE: Child will measure, observe, and use olfactory discrimination.

Make a flower flour dough by using crushed fragrant flower petals. Cut the flower petals with scissors into small pieces and then crush them with the back of a large spoon. The child can help cut and crush the petals before making the dough. To make the dough, have the child help you mix the flour, salt, and water until stiff. Then add the crushed flower petal pieces and mix until crumbly. The child can shape the dough into large beads and pierce them with a pencil. Set the beads outside to dry for several days, or use a wire cooling rack inside. When dry, the child can use a blunt darning needle to string them on yarn to make a scented necklace or bracelet. As a variation, the child can create scented sculptures with the flower petal dough.

271

OUTSIDE ORCHESTRA

Find musical instruments in nature and play them!

OBJECTIVE: Child will use creative-thinking and problem-solving skills.

The child can use creativity to invent instruments from items collected from nature. The child can make rhythm sticks with two sticks, a drum and drumstick with a large rock and a stick, cymbals with two flat rocks (being careful of fingers!), or a shaker by placing acorns inside an oatmeal box or paper bag.

SUN PRINTS

272

Make shape tracings using dark paper and the sunshine!

 WHAT YOU'LL NEED: Dark construction paper, rocks, assorted shape objects (comb, scissors, spoon, etc.)

OBJECTIVE: Child will experiment and observe changes.

On a sunny (not windy!) day, the child can place a dark piece of construction paper outside on the ground in a sunny place. Have the child weight the corners of the paper down with rocks. The child can choose objects to place on top of the paper for printmaking. After several hours, the sun will fade the paper, leaving a darker impression of the objects behind. The child can make prints of individual items on single sheets of paper or can create a collage print that includes several items on one paper. Discuss the changes of the paper with the child.

273

WIND DETECTIVE

Test the wind's strength with outside items.

 WHAT YOU'LL NEED: Nature items of assorted weights (feather, stick, rock, leaf)

OBJECTIVE: Child will predict, test, and draw conclusions.

On a breezy or windy day, the child can gather together an assortment of natural items and then predict which ones the wind will be strong enough to blow away. The items can be placed on a table or bench one at a time to observe the results. For more challenge, have the child place all the items in a row and test them all at once!

SOUNDS AROUND

Investigate sounds around by listening carefully with your eyes closed!

OBJECTIVE: Child will use auditory discrimination and critical-thinking skills.

Start by playing a guessing game together. While the child's eyes are closed, the adult makes sounds with common items (shaking a key ring, flipping the pages of a book, opening and closing the refrigerator). The child can guess what makes the sound and can also take a turn making sounds for the adult to guess. Then, to add challenge, the child can again close his or her eyes (inside or outside), this time listening to the nature sounds around. After sitting quietly for several minutes, the child can name everything he or she heard. The child can also identify whether the sounds were made by people, animals, nature, or machines.

CHARTING THE WEATHER

275

Keep track of the weather with a weather chart!

WHAT YOU'LL NEED: Long strip of paper, crayons or markers

OBJECTIVE: Child will use observation skills.

Make a chart for recording the weather. Use a long strip of paper and mark off squares. The child can keep track of the weather by observing what is happening outside each day and then drawing a symbol in that day's square for sunny, rainy, cloudy, or snowy, or pasting a weather picture or sticker on the chart. For more challenge, the child can record the weather for a month and then count up and compare how many of each kinds of weather days there were that month.

WORD SEARCH

276

▼▼▼▼▼▼▼▼▼▼▼▼▼▼▼▼▼▼▼▼▼▼▼▼▼▼▼▼▼▼▼▼▼▼

Track down and recognize words all around!

OBJECTIVE: Child will use word recognition and emergent-reading skills.

Challenge the child to find words that he or she can read when you are walking around the house or around the neighborhood. These might be words that the child can sound out and read or words that the child recognizes (like Cheerios or STOP). As a variation, the child can start a collection of pictures and labels of recognizable words. The saved words can be kept in a box or could be used for a word collage. You can also start a "Word Wall," where you list all the words the child can read. As the list grows, the child will feel great accomplishment!

WHAT'S MISSING?

277

▬ ▬ ▪ ▬ ▪ ▬ ▪ ▬ ▪ ▬ ▪ ▬ ▪ ▬

Look at what's there and look again at what's not there!

WHAT YOU'LL NEED: Common household objects

OBJECTIVE: Child will use observation skills.

Use observation skills to play a detective game together. Take turns being the hider and the detective. The hider chooses five items (fork, sock, teddy bear, pencil, key chain) to display on a table for the detective to observe. The detective takes a good look then covers his or her eyes. Now the hider removes one of the objects and hides it out of view! After the object is hidden, the detective uncovers eyes and takes a second look to figure out what the missing item is. To increase the challenge, add items to the table.

278 ASSORTED ASSEMBLAGE OF PAPER

Be a paper detective, and search for a multiplicity of paper types.

OBJECTIVE: Child will use critical-thinking and observation skills.

Challenge the child to find different kinds of paper around the house. How many different kinds can the child find? The child can start a collection of samples of each type of paper, such as writing paper, construction paper, newspaper, wrapping paper, paper bag, paper towel, toilet paper, cardboard. The child can categorize the papers, choosing the classification system (shiny and rough, printed and blank, etc.). The activity can be ongoing as the child continues to discover more and different kinds of paper all around.

WEATHER BAND 279

Listen to the outside sounds and play that tune again!

 WHAT YOU'LL NEED: Instruments from activities 96 and 363, household items (broom, cardboard tubes, unsharpened pencils)

OBJECTIVE: Child will use creative-thinking, listening, and observation skills.

The child can listen to the sounds that weather makes and try to re-create the natural sounds using handmade instruments and common household items. The child can use a toilet paper tube maraca to imitate rain sounds, two pencils used like drumsticks might imitate rain dripping sounds. The wind might be imitated by humming into a kazoo, blowing through a paper towel tube, or sweeping with a broom. The child might want to record the weather sounds created or make up a story to tell with the weather sound effects.

280 I HEAR WHERE YOU ARE!

Play a listening and locating game.

 OBJECTIVE: Child will use listening skills.

Invite the child to sit in the middle of a room with eyes closed. Explain to the child that you are going to tiptoe to some part of the room and then make a sound. When you make the sound, the child should point to the place the sound is coming from—still with his or her eyes closed. The child can then look to check. Play again or trade places!

WINDOWS ON THE WORLD 281

Make a window picture and open the windows to see outside!

 WHAT YOU'LL NEED: Stiff paper, scissors, small pieces of drawing paper, tape, crayons or markers

OBJECTIVE: Child will use artistic expression to record personal observations.

The adult can create the building for the child's window views. Make the building from stiff paper by cutting a number of windows in it. Make the windows by cutting squares or rectangles on three sides so that the windows can open and close, much like an Advent calendar. The child then creates all the outside views by drawing pictures of outside things on pieces of paper just slightly larger then the window openings. The child can draw trees, animals, sky, clouds, and other things that we see when looking out a window. (The child can look outside a window for research!) Help the child tape the pictures behind the windows. The child can then open and close the windows to reveal the outside views.

BETWEEN YOU AND ME—RELATING & DISCUSSING!

Communication is basic to life! Children are natural communicators. Communication is essential to well-being, sense of self and community, and intellectual growth. Children quickly learn to make a message clear when they need to express themselves. When the idea is important, the impetus to communicate becomes more urgent! As children participate in meaningful activities, their language skills grow and their thinking deepens. In turn, as their language becomes richer they are stimulated to think in new ways. Adults need to provide rich experiences that are interesting to the child and that validate the child's growing voice through discussion—which will in turn spark both verbal and intellectual growth in the child.

282   NIGHT SOUNDS

Listen carefully and quietly for nighttime noises.

OBJECTIVE: Child will use observation and critical-thinking skills.

Sit quietly together in a darkened room and listen to the nighttime sounds in the house. Share ideas and talk about what might be making each sound, whether it is also heard in the day, and if it sounds the same in the day. Nighttime sounds can also be listened to and explored sitting quietly in the backyard. To carry the exploration further, record some of the various nighttime sounds together to listen to again during the daytime.

SAY IT IN A LETTER

*Write a letter and send it to someone dear,
whether far or near!*

WHAT YOU'LL NEED: Paper, pencil or markers, envelope, stamp. Optional: Tape, tape recorder

OBJECTIVE: Child will use language skills and experience words that can be written down and recorded.

Invite the child to write a letter to a grandparent, relative, friend, or neighbor. The child can dictate the letter to the adult or can write independently and use invented spelling to write down ideas. The child can fold the letter, put it in the envelope, seal it, and put a stamp on. After the adult addresses the letter, the child can decorate the back of the envelope. When the letter is signed, sealed, and ready to go, take a walk together to the nearest mailbox and drop it in! For a variation, next time send a tape-recorded letter. The child can share adventures and news by recording the news and sending off the tape.

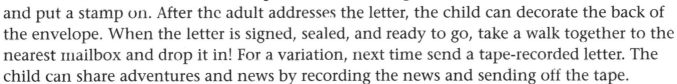

WEATHER WONDERINGS

284

Play a weather wardrobe game.

WHAT YOU'LL NEED: Magazine pictures showing people dressed for different kinds of weather and involved in activities that depict different weather conditions

OBJECTIVE: Child will use critical-thinking and language skills.

Gather together an assortment of magazine pictures that show people dressed in clothing or engaged in activities for a variety of weather conditions. Then take turns describing a weather condition to one another. For example, one person describes the condition: It's very chilly, and rain is coming down. The other person picks a picture that shows the appropriate clothing or activities for that weather and explains the choice.

285 THREE THINGS STORIES

*Put people, places, and things together
in new and unusual ways!*

WHAT YOU'LL NEED: Pictures of people, places, and things cut from magazines;
nontoxic white glue; white paper; 3 bags; marker

OBJECTIVE: Child will use creative-thinking, critical-thinking, and language skills.

The adult gathers together an assortment of pictures of people, places, and things cut
from magazines. Mount the pictures on white paper. Include as
wide a variety of subjects as possible. After all the pictures are
cut, mounted, and gathered, invite the child to sort the pictures
into three piles, one for people, one for places, and one for
things. Once sorted, place each of the piles into a
paper bag, and label the bags. Take turns making up
people, place, and thing stories by choosing one picture from each category and telling ways the three
pictures go together. The reasons can be realistic or
entirely fanciful! To encourage fantasy, the adult can start
the game, giving examples for how the first three things might go
together in a story. After the storyteller has explained the ways the pictures go together, the
listener can ask three questions of the teller to elicit more details. To simplify the game, use
only two categories: people and places or people and things.

By words the mind is winged.
Aristophanes

286 PEANUT BUTTER PLAYDOUGH

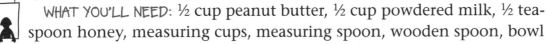

Make, mold, and munch playdough!

 WHAT YOU'LL NEED: ½ cup peanut butter, ½ cup powdered milk, ½ teaspoon honey, measuring cups, measuring spoon, wooden spoon, bowl

OBJECTIVE: Child will measure, experiment, and observe.

Start by washing and drying hands thoroughly! The child can then help to measure the ingredients into the bowl and mix them up. (Have extra powdered milk available in case dough is too sticky). When the dough is malleable, the child can experiment with it—making shapes and sculptures. And fingers can be licked too!

PICTURE THIS

287

Draw one picture, tell two stories!

 WHAT YOU'LL NEED: Paper, markers or crayons

OBJECTIVE: Child will use creative-thinking and language skills.

Take turns drawing pictures to use for story starters. When a picture is finished, the person who drew it (adult or child) tells about the picture and makes up a story to go with it.

 Then the listener makes up an entirely different story about the same picture! For more challenge, instead of drawing two separate pictures, take turns drawing one picture together! Plan out what will be in the picture and who should add what where, or just take turns making additions to the drawing. When the cooperative picture is done, use it as a story starter for two different tales.

WHAT'S WHOSE JOB?

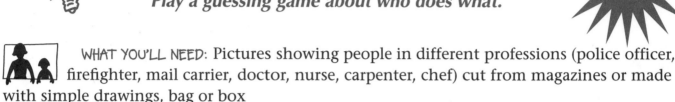

288

Play a guessing game about who does what.

WHAT YOU'LL NEED: Pictures showing people in different professions (police officer, firefighter, mail carrier, doctor, nurse, carpenter, chef) cut from magazines or made with simple drawings, bag or box

OBJECTIVE: Child will use critical-thinking and language skills.

Gather together pictures of professionals at work or in different uniforms that show what their jobs are. Put all the pictures into a bag or box. Take turns pulling a picture out of the bag or box. The person who has chosen a picture looks at it but doesn't let the other person see it. The adult or child who has chosen the picture then tells about the person's job and what kind of tasks they do without mentioning the name of the job or the profession. The other person guesses the profession from the description. After playing, invite the child to share more ideas about different jobs people have. For further discussion, read a book together about jobs and talk about the kinds of work that both men and women can do.

289

TELEVISION TALKS

Don't just watch; watch and talk!

OBJECTIVE: Child will use critical-thinking and language skills.

Talk to the child about the programs or videos the child watches to make the TV viewing active. The adult can ask questions such as: What do you think will happen next? What do you think about what he did? Do you agree with that? Ask questions after the program also, for example: What did you see? What would you have done if you were there? What did you like? What didn't you like? Why?

290

A RING OF THINGS

Create loop books out of pictures of things that go together.

WHAT YOU'LL NEED: Index cards, hole punch, nontoxic white glue, scissors, magazines, large key ring or binder ring or shower curtain ring. Optional: Crayons, stickers, camera

OBJECTIVE: Child will categorize, and use critical thinking and language skills.

If possible, have the child punch holes in the corner of the index cards to serve as the pages of the book. Otherwise, the adult should punch the holes. The child chooses the categories for the looped books, such as dogs, red things, baby animals, hats, or things I like to eat. After selecting a category, the child searches magazines for pictures that fit the category. The pictures can be cut or torn out and glued onto the individual cards. All the cards in one category are looped together with

a ring. After a looped book has several pages, encourage the child to share the book and tell about what is in it and why they go together. Looped books can be ongoing—the child can continue to add pictures. The child can also add to them by drawing on the cards, putting stickers on them, or even taking photographs of items that fit in the category!

Better to have education than wealth.
Welsh proverb

STORY INNOVATION

291

Change the words, change the meaning, change the story!

WHAT YOU'LL NEED: Optional: Paper, crayons or markers, pencil

OBJECTIVE: Child will use critical- and creative-thinking skills.

Create a new version of an old story or song by replacing original words with new ones. Choose a story or a storybook of a song that has a predictable, repeating verse (such as "The Old Woman Who Swallowed a Fly" or "Old MacDonald"). Read it together and talk about the words that could be changed and how the meaning would change as well. Invite the child to think of different words to use within the repeated phrases. The child can volunteer each new word during a rereading, or before reading the story again brainstorm with the child to come up with groups of words with a related theme. For more challenge, the child can draw pictures to accompany the new version, and the adult can write the new verse!

292

FREEZE DANCING

Dance, prance, jump, and hop, then turn off the music, freeze and stop!

OBJECTIVE: Child will use creative-thinking and listening skills.

Play music or sing a song for the child to dance to. The child can also jump, hop, skip, sway, or move to the music in any way. Explain to the child that while the music plays he or she should keep moving, but as soon as the music stops the child freezes and becomes a statue! As soon as the music begins again, the frozen statue melts back into motion. To make the game more challenging, encourage the child to imagine and report on the kind of statue he or she has frozen into each time the music stops.

PUPPET PROBLEMS

293

Help out perplexed puppets puzzled with problems!

WHAT YOU'LL NEED: See activities 78 and 94

OBJECTIVE: Child will use critical-thinking and language skills.

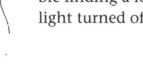

To make simple puppets, refer to activities 78 and 94. Pose a problem that two puppets might be having for the child to help solve. The child can act as an intermediary for two puppets, each of whom the adult is speaking for. Or the adult can use one puppet and the child the other, and the two puppets can talk to each other to work out the dispute. To make the activity easy, present problems that are not interpersonal, for example, one puppet might have trouble finding a lost toy or be afraid of sleeping with the light turned off—so the puppet needs advice!

294

SILENT SINGING

Sing a song silently!

OBJECTIVE: Child will use critical-thinking and observation skills.

Choose action songs with plenty of gestures for silent singing. Together, sing the songs out loud the first time around, accompanying them with all the gestures. Then, "sing" the songs silently, using all the gestures but only mouthing the words. Songs can be silently "sung" together in a "chorus" or can be "sung" solo as adult and child take turns silently singing songs (with gestures) for one another to guess. Some good songs with many gestures to start with are "The Eensy Weensy Spider," "Head and Shoulders," "Open, Shut Them," and "Five Little Ducks."

295

FLASHLIGHT ART IN THE DARK

Shine colored light to glow and gleam and blend and beam.

WHAT YOU'LL NEED: Flashlights, colored cellophane, rubber bands

OBJECTIVE: Child will experiment and observe.

Cover the top of a flashlight with colored cellophane and secure it with a rubber band. Cover the top of a second flashlight with a different color of cellophane. When the flashlights are turned on, the light that shines through will make a tinted reflection as it hits the wall or ceiling. The child can explore the colored reflections in a darkened room and can also experiment with color mixing using beams of tinted light. The child can use the two flashlights and direct them so the beams collide, or the adult and child can each shine a beam, dancing the lights together and apart.

296

REAL OR MAKE-BELIEVE?

Listen and ponder whether stories could really be real!

OBJECTIVE: Child will use critical-thinking skills.

Share fiction and nonfiction books with the child. After reading a story or a section of a book, ask the child to determine whether the tale was real or make-believe. Encourage the child to explain the reasoning behind the determination. For a variation, look at magazine pictures together and take turns making up real and make-believe statements about the pictures. One person makes a statement and the other guesses whether the information stated is real or make-believe.

297

BIRD WATCHING

Go birding with homemade play binoculars!

WHAT YOU'LL NEED: Toilet paper tubes, nontoxic white glue, hole punch, thick yarn

OBJECTIVE: Child will use observation and language skills.

To make binoculars, the child can glue two toilet paper tubes together. The adult will probably need to punch holes on the outside edge of each tube (if the child can, let him or her do it). Cut a length of yarn, and thread an end through each hole. Tie a knot on each yarn end to create a strap. The child can put the binoculars over his or her head so they're ready to use when a bird is spotted! Take a walk to the park or go outside in the yard to look for birds to observe. Encourage the child to describe any birds that are sighted while birding. The child can tell about the size and color of the bird, how it flies or walks, and where it lands. The child can also imitate the bird's movements and make guesses and hypothesize

about what the birds are doing and why. For further bird study, check out a children's library book on backyard birds and look at the pictures together to find out more about the birds you observed while birding.

SAVOR THE FLAVOR

298

▼▼▼▼▼▼▼▼▼▼▼▼▼▼▼▼▼▼▼▼▼▼▼▼▼▼▼▼▼▼▼▼

Take a taste test and tell what tastes best!

WHAT YOU'LL NEED: Variety of food snacks with different kinds of tastes (pickle, lemon slice, potato chip, marshmallow). Optional: Blindfold

OBJECTIVE: Child will use observation and language skills.

Have everyone wash hands first! Gather together food samples with a variety of sweet, salty, and sour flavors. The child can take a taste test with eyes closed or even blindfolded. Invite the child to guess what each food is and also to describe how it tastes using flavor words. For a variation, the child can taste, compare, and describe foods with different kinds of textures (sticky, crunchy, smooth).

299

MIRROR, MIRROR

●●●●●●●●●●●●●●●●●●●●●●●●●●●●●●●

Look at me and tell me what you see!

WHAT YOU'LL NEED: Full-length mirror, tape recorder, blank tape

OBJECTIVE: Child will use observation, critical-thinking, and language skills.

Stand together in front of a full-length mirror and take turns describing what you see. Challenge the child to continue to add more and more details to the observations. For more fun, make a tape recording of the observations. Then, later the same day, return to the mirror and play back the tape. Note if anything has changed or if there are additional observations that were not noticed and recorded during the earlier viewing.

LIKES AND DISLIKES

300

*Create a collage chart to spark discussion
of likes and dislikes.*

WHAT YOU'LL NEED: Paper, marker, old magazines, scissors, nontoxic white glue

OBJECTIVE: Child will use critical-thinking and language skills.

Divide a large piece of paper in half and label one side with a happy face and the other side with a sad face. The child can look through magazines for pictures of things he or she likes or doesn't like. The pictures can be cut or torn out and then glued onto the happy or sad side of the paper. The child can share the finished picture and tell about the things on each side and why he or she likes or dislikes each of them. For a simpler variation, look through a magazine together and take turns finding pictures of things that you each like or don't like and telling why.

301

COLLAGE STORIES

*Make up a story from pictures, and make a
picture of the story!*

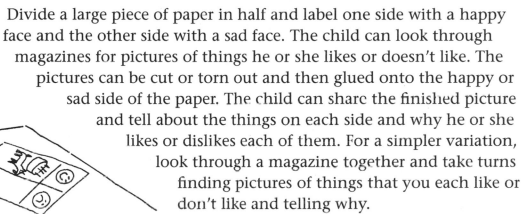

WHAT YOU'LL NEED: Old magazines, scissors, nontoxic white glue, paper

OBJECTIVE: Child will use creative-thinking and language skills.

The child can tear or cut out pictures from magazines and use them to create stories. All the pictures can then be glued onto one piece of paper to create a collage story that contains the whole picture!

302 IMPROMPTU INTERVIEW

Interview a child about the secret of his or her success!

WHAT YOU'LL NEED: Clipboard, paper, pencil, tape player, blank tape

OBJECTIVE: Child will use critical-thinking and language skills.

Pose as a journalist with a notebook and a tape recorder. Ask the child questions about something he or she does well. The interview might center around a single achievement, such as making a playdough sculpture or learning to tumble upside down. Or it could center on a special area of interest or expertise, such as drawing pictures of bugs, singing, or running! Ask for background information as a journalist on a news story would, such as the child's age, what other kinds of things the child  likes to do, what the child likes to eat for breakfast, etc. Ask about the specific reason for the interview, how the child became interested in it, prior experience, and the secret of the child's current success. Ask the child for any advice for others as well. Take notes and also tape-record the interview. When the interview is over, listen to the tape together. Ask the child if there is anything further that needs to be added to the story. If the story is complete, play it again for other family members to hear. The child can then answer any additional questions that come up.

"When I use a word," Humpty Dumpty said in a rather scornful tone, "it means just what I choose it to mean neither more nor less."

Lewis Carroll

MORE TASTING AND TELLING

303

Taste some more and tell about more than taste!

 WHAT YOU'LL NEED: Variety of breads (whole wheat, corn tortilla, bagel, croissant, challah), paper plates

OBJECTIVE: Child will use observation and language skills.

Have everyone wash hands first! Gather several different kinds of bread together to taste and compare. The child can look, touch, and taste each kind of bread. In-  vite the child to share observations about the size, shape, color, and texture of the different breads. How are they the same? How are they different? Encourage the child to describe the taste of each of the breads using descriptive words, such as sweet, chewy, dry, or soft. To explore breads further, go on a shopping excursion to the market or bakery, and choose a new kind of bread together to buy and try!

304

RIDDLE RHYMES

Rum-tum-tiddle, tell me a rhyming riddle!

 OBJECTIVE: Child will use critical-thinking skills and auditory discrimination.

Take turns making up riddles that have rhyming hints for one another to guess. For example: I'm thinking of something that purrs and it rhymes with hat; I'm thinking of something you put on your foot and it rhymes with blue. For a more challenging rhyming riddle variation, tell a riddle without a rhyming clue, for which the answer must be a rhyme. For example, what's a furry pet that purrs and is very large? (A fat cat.)

305

ALL I KNOW!

Tell everything!

OBJECTIVE: Child will use critical-thinking and language skills.

Pick one topic and challenge the child to tell all he or she knows about it. Some topic ideas are dinosaurs, dogs, trees, cookies, pizza, or shoes. The child's ideas can be written down and read back for review. Another list can also be made of things the child would like to know about the topic. After the second list has been made, encourage the child to come up with some ways to find answers to some of the questions on the second list. Make a research plan together. The plan might include observation, asking an expert, or getting a book from the library. Then put the plan into action!

SEQUEL STORIES

306

Imagine what happens after the story ends!

WHAT YOU'LL NEED: Favorite folktale or story

OBJECTIVE: Child will use critical-thinking, creative-thinking, and language skills.

Encourage the child to think about what happens after a favorite story ends. What do the people and animals do next? Do they have any other problems? Adventures? Funny experiences? Do they stay in the same place? Move far away? Go on a vacation? Do they meet any new people? After reading or retelling a favorite story, invite the child to make up and tell a story about what happens after the story ends! For a variation, the child can imagine and make up what took place just before the story began.

MAKE A SIMPLE SOUP!

Shop, prepare, and cook up a simple sumptuous soup!

307

WHAT YOU'LL NEED: 1 can chicken or vegetable broth, 2 cups water, 1 cup tomato juice, ½ teaspoon salt, vegetables (1 carrot, 1 celery stalk, 1 small potato, 1 onion), 1 cup thin noodles, pot, cutting board, knife, pot holders, large spoon, 2 soup bowls, 2 soup spoons

OBJECTIVE: Child will make decisions, follow steps in a process, and observe.

Use the vegetables listed above or make preferred substitutions! Discuss, shop for, and choose the vegetables for the soup together. To prepare the soup, have everyone first wash hands, and then wash the vegetables. The adult can cut up the vegetables while the child is washing the others. Add the vegetables to the broth and simmer until tender. Then add the noodles to the soup and cook several minutes more. When the soup is ready, scoop it into bowls and share the finished product. Discuss how the soup smells as it cooks, and discuss how it tastes!

The human mind is our fundamental resource.
John F. Kennedy

308 VERSION VARIATION

Share and compare different versions of a single story.

WHAT YOU'LL NEED: Several versions of the same story

OBJECTIVE: Child will use critical-thinking and listening skills.

Gather together the same story written by different authors and illustrated by different artists. (Traditional fairy tales told in different versions by different cultures can also be used.) Read the different tellings together. Invite the child to share ideas about what was the same in each of the stories and what was different. The child can also tell about which of the stories was most enjoyable and why. For a more challenging variation, share several different books all by the same author. The child can look for similarities among the different books or draw conclusions about what kind of stories the author likes to write.

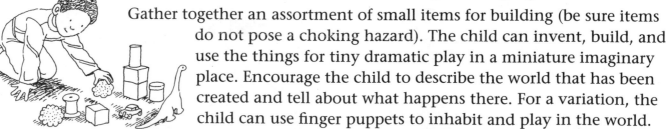

SMALL WORLD 309

Create a diminutive domain with very little things.

WHAT YOU'LL NEED: Small table blocks, thread spools, empty film canisters, cotton balls, construction paper, fabric scraps, small dolls, plastic dinosaurs and animals, toy cars

OBJECTIVE: Child will use creative-thinking and language skills.

Gather together an assortment of small items for building (be sure items do not pose a choking hazard). The child can invent, build, and use the things for tiny dramatic play in a miniature imaginary place. Encourage the child to describe the world that has been created and tell about what happens there. For a variation, the child can use finger puppets to inhabit and play in the world.

310 CHARACTER COMPARISONS

Compare and contrast characters who live in different stories!

WHAT YOU'LL NEED: Two stories

OBJECTIVE: Child will use critical-thinking and language skills.

After reading two different stories, invite the child to talk about the main characters from each of the two stories. Encourage the child to describe ways in which the people or animals were similar and ways that they were different. The child can also talk about how their situations, problems, families, where they lived, or what they liked to eat were similar or different. For more challenge, the child can imagine and describe what each character might have done if he or she were placed into the middle of the other character's story!

FELT BOARD STORY SETS 311

Make story sets to accompany storybooks for active retelling.

WHAT YOU'LL NEED: Favorite storybook, construction paper, markers, scissors, cardboard, nontoxic white glue, sandpaper, felt board, freezer bag

OBJECTIVE: Child will use critical-thinking, sequencing, and language skills.

The adult can create story sets of the child's favorite stories. Make simple drawings to represent the characters and the main props. Cut out and glue the pictures onto cardboard. Glue a piece of sandpaper to the back so the piece will stick to the felt board. Keep all pieces for a story in the freezer bag. The child can use the book with the story pieces—using the book's pictures as clues for what to place on the board.

TOE TALK

Draw tiny toe faces and gather toes together for a talk!

 WHAT YOU'LL NEED: Washable markers

OBJECTIVE: Child will use creative-thinking and language skills.

The adult and child can each draw faces on the bottoms of each other's toes using washable markers. The adult and child (or two children) can then sit on the floor, feet to feet, and make up conversations for their toes to have with one another. For a variation, have knee-to-knee talks, elbow conversations, and finger chats, too!

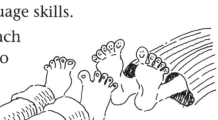

RACING CARS

Create a simple board and play a counting race game with cars.

 WHAT YOU'LL NEED: One die, racetrack made by drawing two or more columns of 20 squares, small cars for game markers

OBJECTIVE: The child will estimate and count.

Each player chooses a column on the racetrack and a toy marker. Then take turns rolling the die, counting the dots on the die, and moving the toy marker the appropriate number of squares. The first player to cross the finish line wins the race. To make the game more challenging, add the requirement that the winner must get the exact number to cross over the finish line! For a variation, racetracks can be made with curving or round tracks instead of straight rows.

CARDBOARD SHAPE FAMILY

Turn circles, squares, and triangles into sisters, brothers, fathers, and mothers.

314

WHAT YOU'LL NEED: Cardboard or tagboard, scissors, nontoxic white glue, fabric scraps, yarn, markers

OBJECTIVE: Child will use creative-thinking, problem-solving, and language skills.

Cut cardboard or tagboard into a variety of sizes of circles, squares, triangles, and rectangles. The child can use the shapes to create the members of his or her family. The child can choose shapes and sizes to glue together to create each person. The child might choose to make very simple bodies, gluing only a circle onto a rectangle or triangle, or he or she may favor more sophisticated people, using a square for a body, a circle for a head, a triangle for a hat, and skinny rectangles for arms and legs. Honor all choices! After the child has created the people, fabric scraps can be glued on for clothing, yarn can be glued on for hair, and faces and other details can be drawn with markers. The child can then tell about the family members created and can also create stories and dialogue.

A learned blockhead is a greater blockhead than an ignorant one.
Benjamin Franklin

WALKIE-TALKIE

315

Make a walkie-talkie and engage in telephone talk!

WHAT YOU'LL NEED: 2 empty cans, electrical tape, large nail, hammer, twine

OBJECTIVE: Child will use language skills.

Use electrical tape to tape the top of each can—to smooth down any sharp edges. The adult or child (with adult supervision) can make a hole in the bottom of each can using a hammer and a large nail. Insert the ends of the twine into each of the holes of the cans. Tie a large knot in the end of the twine on the inside of each can to hold it in place. The adult and child (or two children) can then each take one of the cans and walk away from each other until the line is taut. Using the cans as both a telephone receiver and a mouthpiece, start your walkie-talkie conversations!

316

TELL A SONG

Tell a song story and guess the song.

OBJECTIVE: Child will use critical-thinking, listening, and language skills.

Play a song guessing game together by retelling the stories of familiar songs. Take turns retelling song stories for the other to guess. Use new words to tell the story of a song you normally sing together. For example, a song question might be: What song is about a little girl who brings a fluffy white pet that goes "baa baa" to her school? To give an extra hint to the person trying to guess the song, the person telling the story can hum some of the tune of the song.

SAY IT ANOTHER WAY

317

Find new words to tell the same thing differently.

OBJECTIVE: Child will use critical-thinking and language skills.

Take turns making statements and challenging one another to say the same thing in another way. For example, I went to the park to play—I skipped to the grassy place to have fun. The dog is hungry—Our pet wants food. To simplify, invite the child to replace one descriptive word with another. For example, ask the child to find another word to explain that a cookie tastes good (yummy, delicious, great) or that it would be fun (neat, great, exciting) to go to the park.

318

ACCUMULATING MEMORIES!

Share observations by creating a cooperative cumulative list!

OBJECTIVE: Child will use memory, listening, and language skills.

Make a memory list after a trip to the market, a visit to the park, or just a back-yard adventure. One person reports one thing he or she observed. The other person repeats the first observation and adds another. For example: We saw a caterpillar; We saw a caterpillar and a worm; We saw a caterpillar and a worm and the blue sky. Keep taking turns and adding observations, and see how long a list can be remembered and repeated! When the list gets too long, start another one with observations about a different adventure, and see how long that list can get! To play another version of this game, take turns naming three things you each observed. Then take turns seeing how many of the six things named each person can remember!

319

THAT'S HAPPY, THAT'S SAD

Play a storytelling game with happy, sad, silly, and mad options.

WHAT YOU'LL NEED: Tagboard, scissors, marker, brad

OBJECTIVE: Child will use creative-thinking, critical-thinking, and language skills.

Make a spinner for the game using tagboard. Cut a square out of tagboard, and draw a large circle on it. Then cut a pointer out of the tagboard also. Divide the circle into four sections using a marker. Draw either a happy, sad, angry, or silly face in each section. Attach the pointer to the center of the circle with a brad pierced through both pieces. Now it's time to start the storytelling! Take turns spinning the spinner to tell a story. The first person spins and starts the story. If the spinner lands on a sad face, something that is sad must happen in that part of the story. If the spinner lands on the silly face, something silly has to happen! Continue spinning and adding to the story until the story starts winding down. One person can then end the story, or choose how many turns each person will have before starting the game.

No one is without knowledge except him who asks no questions.
West African proverb

320 WHAT'S IN THE BOX?

▼▼▼▼▼▼▼▼▼▼▼▼▼▼▼▼▼▼▼▼▼▼▼▼▼▼▼▼

Play a mystery guessing game using descriptive hints!

WHAT YOU'LL NEED: Shoe box, assorted common items

OBJECTIVE: Child will use critical-thinking and language skills.

Take turns choosing a mystery item to put in a shoe box. Choose common objects, such as a spoon, a block, a toy car, etc. The person who has chosen the object describes how the object is used—without telling what it is. The other person guesses what the object is! To make the game more challenging, have the child think of an object and describe it!

IMAGINARY KINGDOM 321

■ ■ ■ ■ ■ ■ ■ ■ ■ ■

Invent and design an imaginary land and locale.

WHAT YOU'LL NEED: Water colors, paper, sponge, bowl of water, brush, markers

OBJECTIVE: Child will use critical- and creative-thinking skills.

The child can depict an imaginary place that he or she would like to visit and create a map laying out what goes where. Encourage the child to imagine and describe the details of the imagined place, the people and animals that live there, the homes they live in, and the kinds of trees and flowers that grow there. The child can create the background of the map of the land by painting with watercolors on wet paper. The paper is either dipped in water first or sponged on both sides with a wet sponge. When the paint has dried, the child can draw in the details of the land with markers, showing where the people live, where the houses are, and where the animals roam.

322 COMICAL MAGNETS

▼▼▼▼▼▼▼▼▼▼▼▼▼▼▼▼▼▼▼▼▼▼▼▼▼▼▼▼▼▼▼

Turn Sunday funnies into refrigerator story magnets.

WHAT YOU'LL NEED: Sunday funnies, scissors, nontoxic white glue, tagboard or recycled cardboard, magnetic tape

OBJECTIVE: Child will use creative-thinking, sequencing, and language skills.

For making these magnets, choose a comic that demonstrates obvious action. Cut apart each of the comic boxes and glue them onto a piece of tagboard or the back of a cereal box cut to size. A strip of magnetic tape placed on back of each will turn the comic squares into magnets. The child can put the pictures in sequence on the refrigerator and make up original stories to tell using the pictures. The child can also rearrange magnets into new action sequences and make up different stories. For a variation, make refrigerator magnets using stickers or stamps (canceled) that the child can use for magnetic sorting.

Every child is born a genius.
R. Buckminster Fuller

MY BOUNCY BODY—
MOVING & MANIPULATING!

Young children have bouncy bodies! They wiggle, squirm, crawl, roll, and scoot around. Movement, motion, and manipulation of the objects around them are critical to their growth and physical development. This is how they develop their muscles. They develop the large muscles first, then the small ones, which do fine work such as writing and tying shoes. Being bouncy is also how they express their feelings and moods. Through movement, children develop an understanding of their body in space and what each body part can do. They learn the limits of their abilities, as well. Their successful physical development contributes to their sense of confidence.

ANIMAL MOVES

Wiggle, wriggle, romp, and stomp!

323

OBJECTIVE: Child will use body movements to express ideas.

Invite the child to run, hop, creep, crawl, and "fly" like common animals and insects might. Encourage the child to wriggle across the room or yard like a slithery snake. Challenge the young athlete to jump like a hoppy frog or to trot like a frisky pony. Use descriptive language to help paint a movement picture. For a greater challenge, add more details to each animal story. For example: Can you sneak along like a cat who has just spotted a butterfly, and then show me what the cat will do next?

MIRROR DANCING

324

Watch me watching me in the mirror!

WHAT YOU'LL NEED: Full-length mirror

OBJECTIVE: Child becomes aware of body movements and positions.

Have the child stand in front of a full-length mirror and dance or move using arms and legs. Point out how the arms and legs look as they move. Encourage child to nod and wiggle and explore. When the child becomes aware that what they are watching is the reflection of what they are doing, then place the child in front of you. Explain that you are going to be the mirror and will do exactly what you see the child doing. Copy the child's movement—then trade places and let the child be the mirror!

325

STAY STILL AND MOVE

Frolic and bounce in one place in one space!

WHAT YOU'LL NEED: Masking tape. Optional: Radio, CD, or tape player

OBJECTIVE: Child will use critical- and creative-thinking skills.

Challenge the child to find new ways to move while staying in one place. Give the child masking tape to tape an × on the floor to mark the spot! The child can start off by sitting on the spot. Encourage the child to experiment with different ways to move or dance while sitting. Help the child by offering some suggestions, such as, swaying, twisting, or wiggling. After experimenting with a variety of movements while sitting, invite the child to explore movement possibilities while keeping contact with the spot with a foot, hand, or tummy. Add music to dance on the spot!

326 EXPRESSIVE, IMAGINATIVE PLAY WITH FABRIC

Make-believe fun is found in new forms with fabric.

WHAT YOU'LL NEED: 3 yards fabric

OBJECTIVE: Child will learn how the whole body works together to accomplish a task.

This open-ended, very expressive activity requires imagination on the child's part and guidance from the adult on how to work with the fabric. Have the child take one end of the fabric, and the adult can take the other. Try to make the fabric move, float on air, and turn as you both turn. Explore ways to make the fabric move. After the child has discovered some of the ways fabric moves, try the following activities:

1. Hold the fabric at each end and make waves, like the soft waves on a calm sea. Then make the waves like the huge waves on a stormy ocean.

2. Hold the fabric around each of you. Pretend you are in a boat on a calm sea moving gently with the waves.

3. Pretend you are like a flagpole and the fabric is the flag. Make it move with the wind— both a calm and a wild wind.

4. Pretend the fabric is like a sleeping animal by rolling it into a ball. The child can grasp one end of the fabric and shake it as if the animal is awakened as the fabric is unrolled. The child can also make sounds of an awakened animal.

5. Hold both ends to make the fabric into something like a mountain. Then let go to have the mountain crumble flat.

6. The child can wrap him- or herself in the fabric, and then the child can spin out of the fabric like a top. (Be sure this is done in a safe place.)

7. Stretch the fabric over both of your heads and be like a Chinese dragon in a parade.

OBSTACLES OF COURSE

You never know what obstacle might pop up on this course!

WHAT YOU'LL NEED: 3 cardboard boxes, about 1 yard of fabric, table, masking tape, construction paper, scissors

OBJECTIVE: Child will use arms and legs together to perform a task.

Make paper cones to place along the route to mark the course boundaries. Take a sheet of construction paper, and cut out a half circle. Roll the paper into a cone and tape it. Cut off the top and bottom of one box and turn it on its side. Leave one box open on top for the child to crawl in and out. Cut holes in adjoining sides of the last box. Now design the course, placing the cones to guide the child through the course. The child will spend hours crawling through the course!

PASS THE BEANBAG

Beans, beans, can you throw the beans?

WHAT YOU'LL NEED: 3 old socks (without holes), 3 legs from old nylons, small beans, bucket or 5-pound coffee can, old belt

OBJECTIVE: Child will develop hand-eye coordination.

The child can help make the beanbags. Fill each nylon leg with 1 cup beans. Tie the end of the nylon tightly, and cut off the excess. Place the nylon beanbag inside a sock and tie off the end of the sock tightly; cut off the excess. (Be sure sock material is thick and without holes—small beans can be a choking hazard.) Then find a spot that is out of the traffic area. Place the bucket on the ground. Take three giant steps away from the container and lay the belt down. The child stands behind the belt and tosses the beanbags into the container. Increase the challenge by moving the belt farther away from the bucket.

329

BUBBLE RUN

Long, longer, longest—how far will bubbles fly?

WHAT YOU'LL NEED: Bowl, liquid detergent, glycerin, plastic six-pack ring or plastic berry basket. Optional: String, tape measure

OBJECTIVE: Child will develop coordination.

This is an outdoor activity for a day that is not too windy. Mix three parts liquid detergent and one part water in the bowl. Add a few drops of glycerin to make bubbles stronger. Locate a runway—a spot free of trees, gardens, and fences—where the child can chase bubbles. Using the six-pack ring or the berry basket as a wand, dip ring or basket in detergent

mixture and blow soap bubbles into the air. Encourage the child to run after and catch as many bubbles as he or she can before the bubbles touch the ground. Encourage the child to guess what happened to the bubbles that went up in the air and blew away. Why did some go higher? To make this activity more challenging, use long pieces of string or a tape measure to measure the distances the bubbles traveled. Have your child compare the distances and figure out why some bubbles went only a short distance and some went farther.

Unless you try to do something beyond what you have already mastered, you will never grow.
Ralph Waldo Emerson

330

GO FISH

Catch your favorite fish!

WHAT YOU'LL NEED: A 24- to 30-inch stick, string, tape measure, scissors, needle, thread, fabric glue, 6 inches hook-side Velcro, ½ to 1 yard loop-side Velcro. Optional: hula hoop, marker

OBJECTIVE: Child will develop figure-ground perception (ability to single out one object from a group).

Have the child help tie 24 inches of string to one end of the stick. (Let the child help measure the length with a tape measure.) Cut and fold six inches of hook-side Velcro with the hook-side facing out; sew the ends together. Have the child help tie the hook-side Velcro loop to the string on the stick. Use the pattern above to make the fish, enlarging it if you wish. Cut out two pieces for each fish you wish to make. The child can help trace the fish onto the loop-side Velcro. Glue the two sides together.

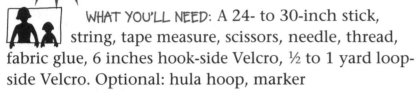

Place the fish on the floor (you can use a hula hoop on the floor for a lake). Have the child use the fishing pole to catch fish. Make the activity more challenging by writing numbers on the fish and/or making the fish different colors. This will add number recognition and color recognition to the game. The child can catch the red number 6 fish or the green number 2 fish.

PLASTIC GROCERY-SACK KITE

331

Let's go fly a kite!

WHAT YOU'LL NEED: Plastic grocery sack, string

OBJECTIVE: Child will develop coordination and hand skills.

Bring together the two handles of the plastic grocery sack and tie them together with a long piece of string. Leave 3 feet of string tied to the handles. Tie a large loop on the other end of the string to provide a loop for the child to hold while flying the kite. Have the child take the kite outdoors and run while holding the string close to the bag handle. As the bag fills with air, the child slides his or her hand down the string to the loop end. Grocery bags make terrific kites and when one tears, just tie on a new one! (Supervise—plastic bags can be a suffocation hazard.)

332

GO TINY TOE BALL GO

Make a tiny Ping-Pong ball go using only a toe!

WHAT YOU'LL NEED: Ping-Pong ball

OBJECTIVE: Child will experiment, observe, and draw conclusions using large- and small-motor skills.

With shoes, socks, or bare feet (all to different effect!) the child uses only toes to get a Ping-Pong ball to go just where it's supposed to go. The goal can be an easy one, such as to get the ball from one side of the room to the other. Increase the challenge by creating an obstacle course with a goal box at the end. The child can experiment with ways to get the ball to move using only toes. The ball can be kicked, tapped gently, or rolled along.

333 MASKING TAPE TRAIL

Tiptoe where the tape trail leads!

WHAT YOU'LL NEED: Masking tape

OBJECTIVE: Child will use large-motor skills and explore balance.

The child can help the adult use masking tape to make a tape trail on the floor—the trail can wind or be straight. The child can then walk, tiptoe, hop, or go backward along the tape trail, trying to stay on the line! For a variation, make masking tape "stepping stones" by creating round shapes, a foot apart, leading in a trail. The child can follow the stepping stone trail by hopping or jumping from "stone" to "stone."

FOIL AND FOAM SCULPTURE 334

Tiny fingers can twist, turn, punch, and poke to make unusual sculptures.

WHAT YOU'LL NEED: Aluminum foil, clean foam tray from fruit or vegetables, foam peanuts, pipe cleaners, construction paper scraps, hole punch

OBJECTIVE: Child will use creative-thinking and small-motor skills.

Child can poke pipe cleaners into an upside-down foam tray. The pipe cleaners can stand free, be punched through foam peanuts, wrapped around molded foil, or looped through paper scraps. The child can mold foil into skinny, fat, or unusual shapes to be added to the sculpture. Foam shapes with pointy ends can also be inserted into the foam base. The child can use a hole punch to turn paper scraps into lace and then loop it around the standing pipe cleaners.

HOOPING IT UP

Jumping through hoops—for a purpose!

WHAT YOU'LL NEED: Hula hoop

OBJECTIVE: Child will learn spatial awareness.

There are lots of ways to play with a hula hoop. Young children find it extremely difficult to use as it was designed, but it is a fun toy to use in many ways! Here are some ways younger children will enjoy playing with it:

1. Lay the hoop on the ground and have the child crawl over one side, through the center, and under the other side.

2. Hold the hoop perpendicular to the ground and have the child walk or jump through it.

3. Lay the hoop on the ground and have the child lie down in the middle. Have the child place his or her head on one side of the hoop and try to pick up the other side with the feet.

4. Encourage the child to roll the hoop and run alongside it, giving the hoop periodic pushes to see how far it will roll.

5. See if the child can spin the hoop.

6. Add the hoop to the obstacle course (see activity 327) or use the hoop with activity 328 to toss beanbags through.

What I have done is due to patient thought.
Sir Isaac Newton

SCARF DANCING

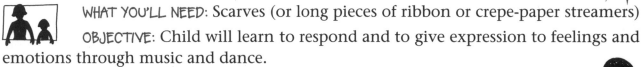

Groove to the music!

WHAT YOU'LL NEED: Scarves (or long pieces of ribbon or crepe-paper streamers)

OBJECTIVE: Child will learn to respond and to give expression to feelings and emotions through music and dance.

Before doing this activity, find a variety of music stations on your radio. Make a list so you can tune them in quickly. Give the child several scarves, and invite the child to move to the music. Change the radio station frequently to provide different feelings of the different types of music. Talk to the child about body movement as the music changes (how different parts of the body can be used to make slow or fast movements). Have the child create a self-expressive dance that incorporates different kinds of music.

SNIP & CUT

Cut! Cut! Cut! All for the fun of cutting!

WHAT YOU'LL NEED: Child-safe scissors, paper plate, variety of items to cut (construction paper, newspaper, plastic straws, fabric scraps, clean foam trays from fruit or vegetables, paper towels, yarn, ribbon). Optional: Paper, nontoxic white glue

OBJECTIVE: Child will use small-motor skills and eye-hand coordination.

Provide the child with an assortment of materials to explore. Encourage the child to cut big pieces, little pieces, fat pieces, and skinny pieces. All the snippings can be collected on a paper plate. If desired, the child can create a collage with all the cut pieces, but no end product is necessary. The child will find cutting for its own sake enticing.

RAIN WALKING

338

It's fun to be outside—in any kind of weather!

WHAT YOU'LL NEED: 2 umbrellas, rain gear

OBJECTIVE: Child will develop coordination and recognition of body movements.

When there is a light rain on a spring day and when the temperature is not too cold, take the child for a rain walk. Both of you will need an umbrella, since sharing is difficult. Wear rubber boots or shoes you don't mind getting wet. As you walk, invite the child to do the following activities:

1. Stomp in puddles.

2. Twirl the umbrella.

3. Talk about where clouds and rain come from.

4. Stick out his or her hand to try to catch a raindrop.

5. Stick out his or her tongue to taste the rain.

6. Listen to the rain hitting the umbrella.

7. If there is wind, talk about how the wind moves the rain and what the wind is doing to the umbrella.

8. Watch water running down the street; talk about why the water moves.

9. Make up a rain and umbrella song.

339 SANDBOX TOYS AND PLAY

Make sandbox toys out of common household items.

WHAT YOU'LL NEED: Plastic margarine tubs, aluminum pie tins, 20-ounce plastic soda bottles, plastic milk jugs, hammer, large nail, wood block, heavy-duty scissors, knife (adult use only)

OBJECTIVE: Child will develop small muscle movements, grasping skills, and pincer control (thumb and forefinger grasping).

Make these sandbox toys for hours of sand fun! Wherever possible, let the child help you make these toys.

1. Use a hammer and large nail to punch holes in a plastic margarine tub to make a colander.

2. Cut a soda bottle in half. The child can use the top half as a funnel, while the bottom can be used as a sand container.

3. Cut a milk jug to make a scoop.

Children can also use foam egg cartons, ice-cube trays, plastic bottles, old pots and pans, scoops, wooden spoons, sieves, sifters, slotted spoons, cake pans, a garlic press, cookie cutters, and rolling pins in the sandbox.

> Without this playing with fantasy no creative work has ever yet come to birth. The debt we owe to the play of imagination is incalculable.
> Carl Gustav Jung

340 WAGON WORK

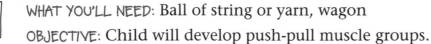

You can take anything with you along this path—as long as you've got your wagon!

WHAT YOU'LL NEED: Ball of string or yarn, wagon

OBJECTIVE: Child will develop push-pull muscle groups.

Lay out a path with the ball of string for the child to follow by pushing or pulling a four-wheeled wagon. Have the child maneuver the wagon along the path, pulling or pushing, depending upon the direction of travel needed. Have the child start with an empty wagon, but as she or he masters the task, you can lay out objects along the path for the child to discover and put into the wagon. Later the child can move the string to make a different pathway. If there is more than one child, the children can take turns pulling each other on the pathway (supervise this closely and be sure the path is on a grassy area).

SHADOW PLAY 341

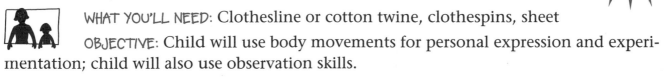

Create shadow shapes, and watch them dance!

WHAT YOU'LL NEED: Clothesline or cotton twine, clothespins, sheet

OBJECTIVE: Child will use body movements for personal expression and experimentation; child will also use observation skills.

Hang a sheet on a line outside on a sunny day (or create an indoor line and shine a light on the sheet). The child can stand in front of the sheet so that the child's body casts a shadow on it. Encourage the child to experiment with shadow shapes. Can the child make a tall skinny shape? a tiny round shape? a fat wide shape? a shape with holes in it? How does the shape change as the child moves closer and farther from the sheet? For a variation, play different kinds of music and have the child invent shadow dances.

SPLATTER PAINTING

Sprinkle, splatter, and scatter colorful drips and drops!

WHAT YOU'LL NEED: Newspaper, tape, large sheet of white paper, tempera paint, plastic bowls, brush

OBJECTIVE: Child will experiment, observe, and draw conclusions while exploring personal expression.

Beware—this is a very messy project! This can be done outside on a calm day or inside. If inside, spread out plenty of newspaper on the floor and tape it down. Place paper in the middle of the newspaper and tape it down. Set the bowl filled with paint on the newspaper. The child can dip a brush into the paint and then, from a standing position, splatter and sprinkle paint drops. After exploring with the paint, encourage the child to experiment. What happens if the brush is shaken softly? What happens if it is shaken harder? Does the child notice a difference if paint is sprinkled from high up or down low?

DEEP DIRT DIGGING

Get down and dirty and explore what's deep below!

WHAT YOU'LL NEED: Old clothes, rubber boots, digging tool (child-size shovel, trowel, old spoon), strainer, pail, plastic tub, water

OBJECTIVE: Child will use large- and small-motor skills when exploring.

A sunny day, old clothes, and an open dirt area are a perfect combination for muddy exploration. The child can use the digging tool to shovel dirt into a plastic tub, then add water for a muddy mix. The mud can be strained. The child can pour water into the hole as part of the play—make a small backyard pond! When the play is over, the child can scoop the mud back into the hole and pat it back down.

WET & WILD!

Squeeze, squirt, and scoop the water!

WHAT YOU'LL NEED: 2 large pans or bowls, large sponge, baster, dishpan, dish detergent, plastic measuring cups, wire whisk, containers, squeeze and squirt bottles, scoops, funnels, ladles, newspaper

OBJECTIVE: Child will develop small-muscle skills. (These are called fine-motor skills.)

Water play can happen constructively in several ways, but the best way to start is with a few of the items mentioned above; too many objects in the water create confusion. Young children also have a tendency to try everything at once if the tub is full, rather than working in an organized way, slowly acquiring skills. (Always supervise children around water.) These are great outside activities, so have the child put on a bathing suit and splash away!

1. On one day, place the sponge, the baster, and two pans outside. Fill one pan with water. (If you decide to do this inside, place bowls in a large dishpan and place newspaper underneath the dishpan to absorb water.) Encourage the child to move the water from one container to the other with the sponge and then with the baster.

2. On another day, fill ⅓ of the dishpan with water and put in five drops of dish detergent. Add the measuring cups, the wire whisk, and the scoops. As your child pours, stirs, and measures, bubbles begin to appear on the surface of the water, creating interesting effects. (Put a thick towel or newspaper under the dishpan if you are inside.)

3. On another day, fill ⅓ of the dishpan with water and give the child a squeeze bottle (an empty dish detergent bottle) and a spray bottle. Have the child fill the bottles as he or she wants and spray the water back into the dishpan. (Have towels around the space to lessen the mess if inside the house.)

4. Another day, fill ⅓ of the dishpan with water and give your child a funnel, containers, scoops, and ladles.

CALL OUT AND DO

345

Hop, skip, and jump to the music!

WHAT YOU'LL NEED: Radio or tape player and taped music

OBJECTIVE: Child will develop large-muscle control, an awareness of how the body works together, and listening skills.

This activity is for those children who can do the activities listed below. The adult will be the caller, and the child will be the doer. Set the activity to music for lots of fun! Select a radio station that has a variety of music selections or use a musical tape. Call all the activities listed in random order: gallop, skip, jump, hop, leap, crawl, stomp, fall, spin, run, roll, skip, squat, bend, stoop. To make it more challenging, give the child a sequence of steps, such as squat, crawl, and roll. Have the child do them in sequence several times. Then change the sequence of steps.

346

MIME

Talk—without using any words!

WHAT YOU'LL NEED: Television

OBJECTIVE: Child will use his or her body to express ideas and feelings.

Show the child mime by turning off the sound of the television and watching a show. Talk about what the child thinks is happening in the silent story. Discuss how people talk with their hands and body expressions—words are not the only way we communicate. Have the child demonstrate sad, happy, mad, scared, and surprised with body movements and facial expressions. The adult can tell a story using facial expressions and body movement. Encourage the child to tell what he or she thought the story was from reading your body movements. Have the child tell a story in the same way—suggest a familiar fairy tale.

TENNIS BALL AND ALUMINUM CAN BOWLING

See how many cans you can knock down with one roll!

WHAT YOU'LL NEED: 15 empty aluminum soda cans, small beans, masking tape, tennis ball, old belt

OBJECTIVE: Child will practice balance and develop hand-foot-eye coordination.

Fill the aluminum soda cans half-full with beans—child can help if supervised carefully (beans can be choking hazards). Place tape over the holes in the tops of all the cans—tape them well. Have the child place the cans in a triangle. Put down the belt for a throw line, about three to four feet from the cans. Have the child use the tennis ball to bowl. Move the belt closer or farther away, depending on the child's skill level. It is important that the child

be successful in knocking down the cans, so it is better to start closer and move back. If the tennis ball does not knock the cans over, pour out some of the beans to make them lighter or try a heavier ball. To make this more challenging, put numbers on the cans and keep track of the points the child makes each time he or she knocks over the cans. You can make each can a point or, if the child can add, put a different number on each can.

The secret of education lies in respecting the pupil.
Ralph Waldo Emerson

348 MAILING TUBES AND BALLS

Pick which ball fits in each tube.

WHAT YOU'LL NEED: 3 or 4 mailing tubes with different diameters, balls (Ping-Pong ball, foam ball, small rubber ball, tennis ball), large basket (Note: If you cannot find mailing tubes, PVC pipe works well.)

OBJECTIVE: Child will predict spatial relationships and test out predictions.

Store the balls with the mailing tubes in a basket. At first, have the child pull out a tube and choose which ball will roll through the mailing tube selected. As the child develops skill at accurately selecting a ball and tube of the correct size, have the child place a smaller tube inside a larger tube and again select a ball to see if it will roll through both tubes.

TRAIN ENGINES AND CARDBOARD BOXCARS 349

Make a choo-choo train in your own backyard.

WHAT YOU'LL NEED: 6 or 7 large cardboard boxes (big enough for child to get into), clothesline rope or strong nylon twine

OBJECTIVE: Child will develop spatial judgment.

Large empty boxes draw young children. Place the boxes outdoors in a shaded area, and encourage the child to make a train. Help the child tie the boxes together with the rope. The child can pretend to be the engine and pull the boxcars around the yard. If the child wants to be the engine but be inside the lead box, cut a large hole in the box bottom to let the child pull the train from inside the box. As the child plays, encourage him or her to observe distances—how close they are to the tree, how far they have moved, etc.

350

LOOP-DE-LOOP BALL

Catch the loops—it is fun and easy!

WHAT YOU'LL NEED: 8 pairs of old clean pantyhose, scissors

OBJECTIVE: Child will learn hand-eye coordination and where their body is in space and in relation to other objects.

This nylon loop ball is easy for young children to catch because it gives them handles that can be grasped and tossed easily. Because it is soft and flexible, it is excellent for younger children who need further development of the muscles of the hand, wrist, and arm. The ball also can be washed in the washing machine and dried in the dryer.

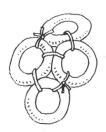

Instructions to make the ball—let the child help you make it wherever possible:

1. Cut off each pantyhose leg at the top of the thigh and at the ankle. You should have 16 legs.

2. Roll each leg in a loop by pulling one end of the stocking up one of your arms, above the elbow, and rolling it back down. Roll all 16 legs in this way.

3. Cut 3-inch-long pieces of stocking from the leftover pantyhose to make ties. You will tie the loops together with these.

4. Assemble the 16 loops by tying them to the other loops at four or five points, until all loops are tied together in the shape of a ball. If each loop is thought of as the face of a clock, all the loops will be tied together by wrapping them to each other at 3, 6, 9, and 12.

351

PARACHUTE PLAYING

Don't let the parachute touch you—run under and back before it falls to the ground!

WHAT YOU'LL NEED: A large round tablecloth, 4 or 5 small balls

OBJECTIVE: Child will estimate and explore how fast they can move.

This is such a fun activity your child will want to do it over and over. It is an activity, however, that lends itself to more than one child being involved. Place the round tablecloth on the floor. Kneel down and hold one side. Have your child kneel and hold the another side. Have you and your child rise at the same time, raising your arms as you rise, lifting the tablecloth over the child's head. Do this several times—up and down—to see how well the tablecloth is held up by the air beneath it. Then let it float to the ground. If there is more than one child, have one child at a time run underneath the tablecloth when it is held at its highest point. After the child understands how the parachute works, start using the balls. Both of you stand holding the sides of the parachute and toss balls into the middle of the cloth. Quickly toss the parachute up and down, trying to keep the balls in the center of the cloth. This is a challenge as the balls go everywhere.

Vision is the art of seeing the invisible.
Jonathan Swift

SHAPING UP

352

Mold yourself into any kind of shape.

WHAT YOU'LL NEED: Large towel

OBJECTIVE: Child will learn that each side of the body is different, but that each side can do the same thing.

Do this activity on a large towel (or on a carpet). Have the child lie on the floor. Then give suggestions about how the child can move his or her body into different shapes. Here are some suggestions for shapes: round, flat, wide, narrow, long, short, fat, thin, pointed, crooked, square, heart shaped. Along with learning about his or her body, the child can begin building a vocabulary of descriptive words. To increase the difficulty of the activity, if the child knows the letters of the alphabet, challenge the child to become letters with his or her body.

353

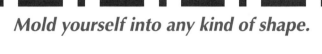

TINY TAPPING

Tap a tiny tune with finger cymbals.

WHAT YOU'LL NEED: Metal bottle caps, hammer, nail, elastic, tape or CD player

OBJECTIVE: Child will explore rhythm, beat, and personal expression through the use of small-motor skills.

To make the cymbals, the adult punches a hole in the center of a metal bottle cap with a nail (be sure the bottle caps have no sharp edges). Cut a piece of elastic about two inches long and thread one end through the hole in the cap. Tie the ends in a knot. Make another in the same way. The child can slip the cymbals onto thumb and forefinger and tap them together to make up a rhythm or to play along with a cassette or CD.

354 WOODWORKING

Build your own creations out of wood.

 WHAT YOU'LL NEED: Thick towel, 4×12×1-inch board, hammer, roofing tacks or other large-headed nails, soft-wood scraps (white pine is best), containers for nails, laundry basket

OBJECTIVE: Child will develop fine-muscle control.

Woodworking is a classic activity, but it is often avoided with young children. Properly supervised, woodworking is among the most enriching activities young children can do—it teaches many skills. It is, as you'll find, one of childrens' favorite activities. Place the towel on the floor in a very low traffic area (outside on a picnic table would also be a good spot). Fold the towel into a thick pad. Place the board on the towel. This is the child's workbench. Make sure the child understands what a workbench is—a place to work. Nails are not to be hammered into the workbench. On the workbench, the child can hammer roofing tacks into a wood scrap. In doing this, the child will be practicing hitting the head of the nail and developing fine-motor skills. Roofing tacks are ideal because the head is large and the nail shaft is short. This makes it easier for the child to be successful. Next, give the child longer nails that allow him or her to nail pieces of wood together, creating various constructions from the wood scraps. It is not important that the constructions be anything—the goal is in the process of building, not in the final outcome!

DRIVING AROUND TOWN

Add spice to running and jumping with a little bit of fantasy.

WHAT YOU'LL NEED: Cardboard box, scissors, child-size broom or long wrapping paper tube, paper bag, markers, construction paper, nontoxic white glue, twine, newspaper. Optional: Paint, sock, felt scraps, fabric glue

OBJECTIVE: Child will use body movement as part of dramatic play.

Create cars for driving and horses for riding and then let children go to town in a backyard or outdoor area with plenty of room to move around. To create a car, cut the bottom and top off a cardboard box. Cut a large armhole in opposite sides of the box. The car can be painted on the outside if the child wants, and car details (headlights, bumper) can be added. The child can then step into the car, put arms through the sides and, holding the bottom edge, drive around. To create a horse for romping, have the child draw a horse face on a paper bag. Draw ears on the bag or make construction-paper ears to glue on. (An old sock can also be used as an alternative for the horse's head. The horse's face can be drawn with a permanent marker or glued on with felt pieces.) Fill the bag with crumpled newspaper and place it over the end of a child-size broom. Securely tie the paper-bag head to the broom with a piece of twine. Tie the two free ends of the twine together to make reins so the child can guide the horse when riding it!

356 GARDENING IN A TIRE

Plant a seed and help it grow into your very own plant.

WHAT YOU'LL NEED: Old tire, garbage bag, potting soil, trowels, seeds, watering can

OBJECTIVE: Child will enhance physical development by squatting, bending, stooping, carrying, and digging.

This activity is best kept simple—plant one kind of seed at a time. Help the child select a plant that you know is hardy and easy to tend. Beans and squash both grow well. Choose an out-of-the-way place in the yard that gets sunlight half the day. Place the tire on top of the bag. Have the child help you fill the tire with potting soil using the trowels. The child can plant three seeds, according to the package directions. Water the seeds as instructed. When there is about four or five inches of growth, remove two of the plants, leaving the most healthy one. Set up a schedule for watering and weeding with your child. Supervise these activities. Your child will be delighted when the plant bears fruit (or squash!).

357 HAND PUPPET GLOVES

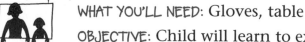

Use only your hands to tell a story—with puppets!

WHAT YOU'LL NEED: Gloves, table

OBJECTIVE: Child will learn to express feelings using hand movements.

Give the child time to experiment using a pair of gloves. The child can start by moving the gloves in front of a mirror to see. The adult should model this. After the child feels comfortable, sit him or her behind a table where the gloved hands can be placed above the table. Again, the adult should model this. Have the child use the gloved hands to express a phrase or word. At first, let the child use words, with the gloved hands supporting the words. Then have the child use only hands to express the words!

SIFTING FLOUR

Playing with flour is like playing with sandy snow!

 WHAT YOU'LL NEED: A dishpan, 2 cups of flour, a scoop, small bowl, squeeze sifter, crank sifter, resealable bag

OBJECTIVE: Child will develop pincer control (use of the thumb and index finger).

Place the flour in the dishpan along with the scoop, the bowl, and the crank sifter. The crank sifter is easier to work than the squeeze sifter. Working in the dishpan, have the child scoop, sift, and dump the flour. After the child has mastered the crank sifter, put it away. Let him or her use the squeeze sifter. (Note: After doing flour play, put the flour in a resealable bag so it will be ready to use next time—but don't use it for cooking.)

TALL WALKING, ON SPONGES

Walk like a robot!

 WHAT YOU'LL NEED: 2 thick car-washing sponges, string

OBJECTIVE: Child will develop leg, ankle, and foot muscles, along with working on balance control during movement.

Tie a sponge to the bottom of each of the child's feet, under the shoes, using the string. Have the child walk on the sponges. Model how to pick up his or her knees while walking so the sponges come off the ground. Encourage the child to "tall walk" by standing up straight (as opposed to bending over) when taking steps. Do this activity over a safe "fall zone" clear of furniture and with thick carpeting. This can also be done outside, but look for a place with soft grass cleared of rocks and other debris.

TONG, TONG, TONGING

See how quickly you can pick up objects using tongs.

360

WHAT YOU'LL NEED: A double-sided dog dish, tongs, everyday objects (dog biscuits, ice cubes, large marbles, rocks, large buttons, leaves, or paper clips)

OBJECTIVE: Child will learn to use and better control small muscles of the hands.

Place a few of the objects (all the same kind) in one side of the dog dish. Have the child pick up the objects on one side of the dog dish and move them to the other side, one at a time. Then have the child move the objects back. Each time you get out the dog dish and tongs, choose a different object to move. As the child gets better at the activity, choose smaller objects to make it more difficult.

361

UPPITY UPPITY

Play uppity uppity—don't let the balloon touch the ground!

WHAT YOU'LL NEED: Balloons. Optional: Wire hangers, pliers, old nylon stocking, masking tape

OBJECTIVE: Child will use observation and large-motor skills.

Blow up two balloons ¾ full—this will make accidental popping less likely. (Always supervise young children around balloons!) In this game, the adult and child each get one balloon, and each one must keep their balloon in the air as long as possible. For a variation, make balloon rackets to bat the balloon back and forth. For a racket, bend a wire coat hanger into a diamond shape and straighten out the hook. Pull an old nylon stocking over the diamond and then wrap the end of the stocking around the straightened hook and tape in place.

POUND, PUSH, PULL, AND PUNCH PLAYDOUGH

Pound out sharp shapes with your own homemade playdough!

WHAT YOU'LL NEED: Salt, warm water, all-purpose flour, large spoon, large bowl, measuring cup, large plastic placemat, container with lid. Optional: Food coloring, garlic press, cookie cutters, plastic knife, tortilla press, cookie sheet, meat hammer

OBJECTIVE: Child will develop the small muscles of the wrists, hands, and fingers.

To make the playdough, have the child help you measure and mix 1 cup of salt in 1 cup of warm water until it is partially dissolved. Add this mixture to 4 cups of flour. Mix with the spoon until well blended and the particles stick together. When the mixture forms a ball, knead it for five to ten minutes. The child may tire of kneading after a few minutes— the adult will need to finish. You can also add food coloring to the balls while you are kneading them if you want different colors of playdough. When you have finished kneading, allow the child to roll, punch, push, pull, and pound using the placemat as the work-space. Not only is this play good for developing the child's hand muscles, but it is also a good outlet for a child's frustration! After each use, store the playdough in the container, keeping the lid on tight when it is not being used. After the newness of the activity has worn off, let the child use some of the optional tools listed above to work with the playdough.

363 STRIKE UP THE BAND!

▼▼▼▼▼▼▼▼▼▼▼▼▼▼▼▼▼▼▼▼▼▼▼▼▼▼▼▼▼▼▼▼▼

Create and play your own musical instruments.

WHAT YOU'LL NEED: Empty long tissue box, rubber bands of different thicknesses, two 4×4×2-inch blocks of wood, sandpaper, nontoxic white glue, thin elastic, jingle bells, scissors, needle, thread, wire coat hanger, metal bottle tops, hammer, nail. Optional: Radio or tape player

OBJECTIVE: Child will learn about rhythm and how to express it with the body.

Guitar: The child can stretch three or four rubber bands over the oval of the tissue box. The child can strum the rubber bands.

Sandpaper Blocks: Cut the sandpaper to fit the blocks of wood. Have the child glue the sandpaper to the bottom of the blocks. Allow the glue to dry. The child can rub the sandpaper blocks together to make a scratchy musical sound. (Caution: Child should not hold the blocks above his or her head while rubbing them together. The grit from the sandpaper can get into eyes.)

Bracelet Bells: Cut eight to ten inches of elastic. Have the child thread the bells along the length and tie them in place. Sew or tie the ends of the elastic together. Have the child wear the bracelet on a wrist or ankle and shake it to the music.

Shaker: Make a shaker by opening a wire coat hanger near the hook. Make holes in the bottle tops and slide them onto the hanger—arranging them back to front—on the bottom of the coat hanger. Most of this the adult will do, but the child can help slide the bottle tops on the coat hanger when the holes are punched. Reclose the hanger. The child can shake the hanger to the music.

Each of the instruments can be played alone or with music from the radio or tape player, or the whole family can get into the swing of it and become a band.

364

BALANCING ACT

Keep cool and steady and balance that bag!

 WHAT YOU'LL NEED: Items for balancing (beanbag, sponge, rubber eraser)

OBJECTIVE: Child will explore balance and movement.

Challenge child to explore balance. With a beanbag on top of his or her head, can the child walk, tiptoe, or run without the bag falling? (See activity 328 for how to make a beanbag.) Can the child walk backward without dropping the bag? What about sideways? Can the child crawl without dropping the bag? The child can also experiment with balance by trying to walk steady with the bag placed on a shoulder, an outstretched arm, a foot, or one bag on each foot! Then try the same activities with the other objects.

FOLLOW THE LEADER

365

Can you do what I do? I can do what you do!

OBJECTIVE: Child will use observation skills.

Follow the child around the house or yard, doing exactly what the child is doing—including running, flapping arms, waving, and hopping. When it is the adult's turn to be the leader, lead the child in some of the following ways: Use facial expressions, such as smiling, frowning, wiggling the nose, or winking; use head movements, such as nodding, twisting, or rotating the head; use finger and hand movements, such as wiggling fingers, snapping, waving, and clapping; use toe and foot movements, such as wiggling toes, tiptoeing, stomping, and sliding feet; and use body movements, such as bending at the waist, squatting, standing on one foot, and wiggling. To add more challenge, repeat combinations of moves, such as winking-waving-stomping-jumping.

INDEX

This index is arranged by skills and abilities.

A Auditory Discrimination
Rhyme Box, 107
Riddle Rhymes, 195
Sound Around, 178
Sounding Off, 22
Water Melodies, 27

B Balance. See Body Coordination

Body Coordination
Balancing Act, 235
Bubble Run, 211
Call Out and Do, 222
Masking Tape Trail, 214
Plastic Grocery-Sack Kite, 213
Rain Walking, 217
Shaping Up, 227
Tall Walking, on Sponges, 231
Tennis Ball and Aluminum Can Bowling, 223

Body Movement
Animal Moves, 207
Balancing Act, 235
Driving Around Town, 229
Expressive, Imaginative Play With Fabric, 209
Gardening in a Tire, 230
Hand Puppet Gloves, 230
Mime, 222
Mirror Dancing, 208
Obstacles of Course, 210
Parachute Playing, 226
Rain Walking, 217
Shadow Play, 219
Tall Walking, on Sponges, 231
Walking Ways, 72

C Categorizing
Catching Raindrops, 9
Dirt Detective, 8
Insects and Spiders, 120

Mood Match, 121
Ring of Things, A, 187

Classifying
Button Sort, 135
Category Compilation, 124
Color Sort, 152
Feel & Sort, 138
Flower Scrutiny, 40
Make a Magnet, 25
Morning, Afternoon & Evening, 149
Nature Collection, 41
Print Matching, 132
Sprigs and Twigs, 157
Take Stock of a Rock, 38
Which One Doesn't Go?, 130

Communication
What I Saw, 170

Comparing
Catching Raindrops, 9
Cooked and Uncooked, 18
Egg Carton Count, 141
Feel & Sort, 138
Flower Scrutiny, 40
Flowing Fountains, 41
Good Vibrations, 39
Hark! I See Bark!, 169
How Big Around?, 38
Leaf Printing, 92
Make a Magnet, 25
Nature Collage, 158
Red, Yellow, and Green, 132
Same as Me, 166
Seed Taste Test, 171
Soapy Similarities, 16
Spoonful of Beans, 123
Take Stock of a Rock, 38
Tape Collage, 80
Wax Paper Window, 168
What Paints How?, 13

What Weighs More?, 111
Who Fits What?, 14
Weigh Away, 42

Comprehension
Sing a Story, 82

Counting
Egg Carton Count, 141
Cookie Counting, 125
Guesstimating Around the House, 114
Insects and Spiders, 120
Racing Cars, 200
Vehicle Tally, 167
What's Inside?, 175

Creative Expression
Foil Sculpture, 86
Goggles for Giggles!, 51
Silhouette Spray, 165
Spoonful of Beans, 123
What I Saw, 170
Windows on the World, 181

Creative Movement
Animal Moves, 207
Dance Streamers, 90
Dancing With Elbows, Noses, or Toesies, 85
Expressive, Imaginative Play With Fabric, 209
How Does an Elephant Dance?, 59
Mirror Dancing, 208
Scarf Dancing, 216
Shadow Play, 219
Stay Still and Move, 208
Tiny Tapping, 227

Creative Thinking
Abstract Art, 53
Acting Out Musical Stories, 57
Animal Pantomine, 96

Beastly Babble, 153
Birthday for a Bear, 59
Body Parts Mix-Up, 137
Building Big Blocks for Big Block Buildings, 58
Building With Boxes, 50
Can You See My Face?, 93
Capture the Wind, 67
Cardboard Critters, 49
Cardboard Shape Family, 201
Collage Stories, 193
Comical Magnets, 206
Cooking Questions, 122
Cork Creations, 61
Crease, Crumple, Crimp & Curl, 90
Cup Puppets, 153
Decorating Me, 82
Foam Boats, 69
Foil and Foam Sculpture, 214
Freeze Dancing, 188
Glue Drops, 99
Hat Parade, 45
Holey Lacies, 78
Imaginary Kingdom, 205
Imaginary Snow, 55
Itty Bitty Teeny Tiny Me, 61
Legendary Lists, 109
Lots of Puppets and Muppets!, 71
Magic Wand, 66
Many Moves, 135
Marshmallow Minaret, 87
Mask Making, 50
May I Serve You?, 51
Me Box, 112
Mood Dance, 152
My Magic Seed, 63
My Private Place, 66
Odds and Ends Weaving, 89
Once Upon a Prop, 87
One Word Drama, 149

Orchestra in One, 73
Outside Orchestra, 176
Paper Wardrobe, 68
Papier-Mâché Pulp Play, 74
Peekaboo Playhouse, 65
Picture This, 185
Ping-Pong Art, 103
Pop-Up Publishing, 134
Pretend Hike, 172
Prolific Puppetry, 60
Prop Prompting, 154
Rock & Clay Creatures and Things, 88
Safe City, 131
Sequel Stories, 196
Singing My Own Song, 138
Sky Dancing, 167
Small World, 198
Snack Face at My Place, 49
Solve the Problem, 136
Stay Still and Move, 208
Stepping Into a Story, 62
Story Cards, 55
Story Innovation, 188
Suit up for Outer Space!, 48
Tell a Tale on Felt, 96
That's Happy, That's Sad, 204
Three Things Stories, 184
Tissue Paper Painting, 98
Toe Talk, 200
Top-Notch Hopscotch, 77
Torn-Paper Pictures, 108
Treasure Hunt, 129
Tube Art, 64
Wax Paper Window, 168
Weather Band, 180
Web Weaving, 44
What Can Shapes Make?, 148
What If?, 144
What Kind of Cat Is That?, 62
What Kind of Creature Are You?, 47
What's Dot?, 53
What's the Question?, 117
Whimsical Words, 58
Wood Scrap Sculpture, 93

Wrapping Paper Stories, 147
Yes or No?, 150

Criticial Thinking
Advice for Mother Goose, 104
Alike & Unalike, 105
All I Know!, 196
Animal Bingo, 119
Assorted Assemblage of Paper, 180
Body Cards, 133
Building Together Apart, 127
Can You Tipplefizzy Me?, 107
Category Compilation, 124
Character Comparisons, 199
Creepy Crawly Exploration, 174
Dry & Spy, 147
Felt Board Story Sets, 199
Hunting for Sounds, 165
I Did Spy, 162
Imaginary Kingdom, 205
Impromptu Interview, 194
Insects and Spiders, 120
It Sounds Like This!, 159
Just Like Me, 110
Legendary Lists, 109
Likes and Dislikes, 193
Local Scene, The, 173
Me Box, 112
Mirror, Mirror, 192
My Hand Is Grand, 140
Night Sounds, 182
Number Riddles, 144
Photojournalism, 106
Puppet Problems, 189
Puzzle Peeker, 110
Riddle Rhymes, 195
Sequel Stories, 196
Sky Dancing, 167
Stay Still and Move, 208
Story Innovation, 188
Real or Make-Believe?, 190
Ring of Things, A, 187
Say It Another Way, 203
Silent Singing, 189
Soak It to Me, 31

Sounds Around, 178
Television Talks, 186
Tell a Song, 202
Tell Me Three Reasons Why, 139
That's Happy, That's Sad, 204
Three Things Stories, 184
Touching the Outside, 118
Version Variation, 198
Weather Wonderings, 183
What Does It Mean?, 108
What Happened Last?, 146
What I Saw, 170
What's Happening Here?, 122
What's in the Box?, 205
What's the Mood?, 145
What's the Opposite, 134
What's the Question?, 117
What's Whose Job?, 186
Where Is It?, 113
Which One Doesn't Go?, 130
Yes or No?, 150

Dramatic Play
All Aboard, 54
Birthday for a Bear, 59
Decorating Me, 82
Driving Around Town, 229
Enchanted Power Cape, 75
Hat Parade, 45
Mask Making, 50
Paper Wardrobe, 68

Drawing Conclusions
Blow or No?, 126
Bug Banquet, 36
Dirt Comparisons, 139
Do Birds Make Birds' Nests Best?, 163
Flowing Fountains, 41
Good Green Growth, 37
Go Tiny Toe Ball Go, 213
How Does My Shadow Grow?, 34
Meltdown, 14
Plant Maze, 35
Puddle Testing, 28

Red, Yellow, and Green, 132
Rolling, Rolling, Rolling, 19
Roll Poll, 112
Seeds on the Up-and-Up!, 164
Seeds, Roots, and Shoots, 30
Shiny Pennies, 154
Sink & Float, 137
Soak It to Me, 31
Soapy Similarities, 16
Sock Walk, 17
Splash Comparisons, 113
Splatter Painting, 220
Tunnel Hole Roll, 146
What Weighs More?, 111
Whirlybird, 85
Wind Detective, 177

E Emergent Reading
Keeping Track of a Tree, 166
Scavenger Hunt, 43
Treasure Hunt, 129
Word Search, 179

Estimating
Guesstimating Around the House, 114
How Many Will Fit?, 25
Parachute Playing, 226
Racing Cars, 200
Spoonful of Beans, 123
What's Inside?, 175

Experimenting
Blowing Beautiful Bubbles, 15
Blow or No?, 126
Box Tower, 124
Bubble Pictures, 79
Colorful Meltdown, 32
Danger! Volcano Explosion Area!, 97
Do Birds Make Birds' Nests Best?, 163
Dip and Dye, 32
Dirt Comparisons, 139
Does It Dissolve?, 19
Dot Painting, 94
Dry & Spy, 147

Egg Carton Count, 141
Explore the Dark, 31
Flashlight Art in the Dark, 190
Floating Boating, 12
Good Green Growth, 37
Go Tiny Toe Ball Go, 213
Leaf and Flower Pressing, 161
Making an Impression, 105
Meltdown, 14
Mingle & Merge Color Splurge, 20
Mix & Fix & Fizzle & Drizzle, 76
Mud Painting, 11
Ocean in a Bottle, 100
Painting With Nature, 33
Paper Caper, 21
Peanut Butter Playdough, 185
Ping-Pong Art, 103
Plant Maze, 35
Print Matching, 132
Reflecting Rainbows, 11
Roller Painting, 92
Seeds on the Up-and-Up!, 164
Seed Taste Test, 171
Shadow Play, 219
Shiny Pennies, 154
Sink & Float, 137
Sock Walk, 17
Splatter Painting, 220
String Painting, 117
Sun Prints, 177
Tool Printing, 103
Tunnel Hole Roll, 146
Watch a Waterwheel Work, 83
Water Viewer, 168
What Weighs More?, 111
Who Fits What?, 14

Exploring
Deep Dirt Digging, 220
Does It Dissolve?, 19
Dot Painting, 94
Flower Scrutiny, 40
Fold and See, Symmetry!, 118
Geoboard, 94

Great & Grand Kitchen Band, 102
Mingle & Merge Color Splurge, 20
Paper Weaving, 115
Parachute Playing, 226
Print Matching, 132
Seed Farming, 169
Tape Collage, 80
Water Melodies, 27
What Paints How?, 13
Whirlybird, 85

Expressing Ideas
Castoff Creations, 47
Look! A Book!, 83

F Figure-Ground Perception
Go Fish, 212

Fine Motor. See Small Motor

Following Directions
Beautiful Beads, 81
Building Bread, 101
Make a Simple Soup!, 197
One Bowl of Ice Cream, Please!, 99
Rebus Receipe, 121
Shape, Paint, and Bake Cookies, 91
Treasure Hunt, 129

G Graphing
Vehicle Tally, 167

Grasping
Sandbox Toys and Play, 218

Gross Motor
Spoon a Ping-Pong Along, 98

H Hand Coordination
Plastic Grocery-Sack Kite, 213

Hand-Eye Coordination
Loop-de-Loop Ball, 225
Pass the Beanbag, 210
Snip & Cut, 216

Hand-Foot-Eye Coordination
Tennis Ball and Aluminum Can Bowling, 223

I Imagination
Telephone Talk, 56
What Kind of Creature Are You?, 47

Interpretive Thinking
Abstract Art, 53
Acting out Musical Stories, 57
Artist Study, 142
Back-to-Back Pictures, 136
Hey! A Survey!, 151
Mood Match, 121
Music Looks Like This, 70
Poem Pictures, 65
Pretend Hike, 172
Rebus Recipe, 121
Sky Dancing, 167
Stepping Into a Story, 62
Walking Ways, 72
What's the Mood?, 145
What the Sunday Funnies Really Say, 57

L Language
Accumulating Memories!, 203
All I Know!, 196
Art Gallery Tour, 142
Bird Watching, 191
Cardboard Shape Family, 201
Character Comparisons, 199
Collage Stories, 193
Comical Magnets, 206
Cup Puppets, 153
Felt Board Story Sets, 199
I'm on TV, 95
Impromtu Interview, 194
Invent Your Own Machine, 75
Just Like Me, 110
Keeping Track of a Tree, 166
Likes and Dislikes, 193
Lots of Puppets and Muppets!, 71

Magic Wand, 66
Magnetic Melodrama, 46
May I Serve You?, 51
Mirror, Mirror, 192
More Tasting and Telling, 195
My Magic Seed, 63
Once Upon a Prop, 87
Peekaboo Playhouse, 65
Photojournalism, 106
Picture Talk, 52
Picture This, 185
Pizza for One, 80
Pop-Up Publishing, 134
Puppet Problems, 189
Prolific Puppetry, 60
Prop Prompting, 154
Ring of Things, A, 187
Savor the Flavor, 192
Say It Another Way, 203
Say It in a Letter, 183
Sequel Stories, 196
Sing a Story, 82
Small World, 198
Snow Cream, 171
Tell a Song, 202
That's Happy, That's Sad, 204
Three Things Stories, 184
Telephone Talk, 56
Television Talks, 186
Tell a Tale on Felt, 96
Tell It to Me, 140
Toe Talk, 200
Walkie-Talkie, 202
Weather Wonderings, 183
What Kind of Cat Is That?, 62
What's in the Box?, 205
What's the Opposite?, 134
What's Whose Job?, 186
Whimsical Words, 58
Wrapping Paper Stories, 147
Yes or No?, 150

Large Motor (also called Large Muscle)
Call Out and Do, 222
Deep Dirt Digging, 220
Go Tiny Toe Ball Go, 213
Masking Tape Trail, 214
Uppity Uppity, 232

Large Muscle. See Large Motor

Letter Recognition
Letter Collage, 163

Listening
Accumulating Memories!, 203
Back-to-Back Pictures, 136
Building Together Apart, 127
Call Out and Do, 222
Favorite Story Cassette, 48
Freeze Dancing, 188
Great & Grand Kitchen Band, 102
Hear the Beat, 156
Hunting for Sounds, 165
I Hear Where You Are!, 181
It Sounds Like This!, 159
Music Looks Like This, 70
Orchestra in One, 73
Poem Pictures, 65
Rhyme Box, 107
Rock & Roll, 160
Singing My Own Song, 138
Tell a Song, 202
Version Variation, 198
Weather Band, 180
What Does It Mean?, 108
Where Is It?, 113

M Matching
Mood Match, 121
Shape Concentration, 114

Math Concepts
What's In, Out, and In-Between?, 143

Measuring
Beautiful Beads, 81
Building Bread, 101
Flower Beads, 176
How Big Around?, 38
Mix & Fix & Fizzle & Drizzle, 76
One Bowl of Ice Cream, Please!, 99
Peanut Butter Playdough, 185

Puddle Testing, 28
Read My Breezeometer, 23
Same as Me, 166

Memory
Accumulating Memories!, 203

N Number Sense
Cookie Counting, 125
How Many Will Fit?, 25

O Observing
Animal Bingo, 119
Artist Study, 142
Assorted Assemblage of Paper, 180
Beautiful Beads, 81
Bird Watching, 191
Bubble Pictures, 79
Bug Banquet, 36
Building Bread, 101
Capture the Wind, 67
Charting the Weather, 178
Circle Search, 160
Colors Around Me, 174
Cooked and Uncooked, 18
Creepy Crawly Exploration, 174
Danger! Volcano Explosion Area!, 97
Decay Away, 21
Deep Dirt Digging, 220
Dirt Detective, 8
Do Birds Make Birds' Nests Best?, 163
Does It Dissolve?, 19
Doodle Drawing, 129
Explore the Dark, 31
Flashlight Art in the Dark, 190
Flower Beads, 176
Flower Scrutiny, 40
Flowing Fountains, 41
Fold and See, Symmetry!, 118
Follow the Leader, 235
Frozen Art, 24
Glue Drops, 99
Geoboard, 94
Go Tiny Toe Ball Go, 213
Hark! I See Bark!, 169
Hear the Beat, 156

How Does My Shadow Grow?, 34
I Did Spy, 162
Invite a Bug Home, 24
It's for the Birds!, 162
Leaf and Flower Pressing, 161
Leaf Printing, 92
Little Piece of Earth, A, 39
Local Scene, The, 173
Make a Simple Soup!, 197
Make Paper, 29
Making an Impression, 105
Meltdown, 14
Mingle & Merge Color Splurge, 20
Mirror, Mirror, 192
Mix & Fix & Fizzle & Drizzle, 76
More Tasting and Telling, 195
Nature Collage, 158
Nature Walk, 159
Night Scenes, 161
Night Sounds, 182
Number Search, 128
Ocean in a Bottle, 100
One Bowl of Ice Cream, Please!, 99
One-Piece Puzzle Match, 109
Opposites Observation, 173
Peanut Butter Playdough, 185
Picture Puzzles, 130
Picture Talk, 52
Ping-Pong Art, 103
Plant Maze, 35
Plant Parts Salad, 170
Puddle Testing, 28
Puzzle Peeker, 110
Rain Painting, 36
Read My Breezeometer, 23
Red, Yellow, and Green, 132
Reflecting Rainbows, 11
Roller Painting, 92
Savor the Flavor, 192
Scavenger Hunt, 43
Seed Farming, 169
Seeds I See, 158

Seeds on the Up-and-Up!, 164
Seeds, Roots, and Shoots, 30
Shadow Play, 219
Shakin' up the Cream, 43
Shape, Paint, and Bake Cookies, 91
Silent Singing, 189
Silhouette Spray, 165
Snow Cream, 171
Sock Walk, 17
Still-Life Paintings, 172
String Painting, 117
Sun Prints, 177
Tool Printing, 103
Uppity Uppity, 232
Watch a Waterwheel Work, 83
Watching Beans Grow, 155
Water Viewer, 168
Wax Paper Window, 168
Weather Band, 180
What I Saw, 170
What Paints How?, 13
What's Happening Here?, 122
What's Missing?, 179

Olfactory Discrimination
Be Still and Smell!, 26
Flower Beads, 176
Inventing Aromas, 10

Ordering
Weigh Away, 42

P Pattern-Making
Look, Listen, and Do, 78
Pretty Pasta Patterns, 116
Pretty Printed Patterns, 77
Shoe Sock Shoe Sock Shoe Sock, 133
Snack Patterns, 125

Personal Experiences
Night Scenes, 161

Pincer Control
Sandbox Toys and Play, 218
Sifting Flour, 231
Tong, Tong, Tonging, 232

Planning
Marshmallow Minaret, 87
Wheel Along, 88

Predicting
Blow or No?, 126
Bug Banquet, 36
Bumping, Bouncing Balls, 16
Cooked and Uncooked, 18
Dry & Spy, 147
Egg Carton Count, 141
Floating Boating, 12
Good Green Growth, 37
It Sounds Like This!, 159
Little Piece of Earth, A, 39
Make A Magnet, 25
Mailing Tubes and Balls, 224
Meltdown, 14
Mingle & Merge Color Splurge, 20
Paper Caper, 21
Puddle Testing, 28
Roller Painting, 92
Rolling, Rolling, Rolling, 19
Roll Poll, 112
Shiny Pennies, 154
Sink & Float, 137
Splash Comparisons, 113
Tunnel Hole Roll, 146
Watch a Waterwheel Work, 83
Weigh Away, 42
What's Inside?, 175
Wind Detective, 177

Problem-Solving
Advice for Mother Goose, 104
Animal Pantomime, 96
Blowing Beautiful Bubbles, 15
Box Tower, 124
Box Town, 150
Building Big Blocks for Big Block Buildings, 58
Building With Boxes, 50
Can You See My Face?, 93
Cardboard Critters, 49
Cardboard Shape Family, 201

Cooking Questions, 122
Dancing With Elbows, Noses, or Toesies, 85
Floating Boating, 12
Foam Boats, 69
Foil Sculpture, 86
Invent Your Own Machine, 75
Itty Bitty Teeny Tiny Me, 61
Many Moves, 135
Marshmallow Minaret, 87
Mud Painting, 11
My Hand Is Grand, 140
Number Riddles, 144
Once Upon a Prop, 87
One-Piece Puzzle Match, 109
One Word Drama, 149
Opposites Observation, 173
Orchestra in One, 73
Outside Orchestra, 176
Photojournalism, 106
Picture Puzzles, 130
Rock & Clay Creatures and Things, 88
Safe City, 131
Secret Sights, 157
Solve the Problem, 136
Spoon a Ping-Pong Along, 98
Stepping Into a Story, 62
Story Cards, 55
Story Switcheroo, 145
Tell Me Three Reasons Why, 139
Top-Notch Hopscotch, 77
Torn-Paper Pictures, 108
Tube Art, 64
What Can Shapes Make?, 148
What Happened Last?, 146
What Would You Do?, 52
What's Dot?, 53
Wheel Along, 88
Yes or No?, 150

Push-Pull Muscles
Wagon Work, 219

S Self-Expression
Foot Painting, 84

Hand Puppet Gloves, 230
Mime, 222
Onstage, 70
Papier-Mâché Pulp Play, 74
Pudding Painting, 95
Strike up the Band!, 234
Tissue Paper Painting, 98

Sequencing
Comical Magnets, 206
Felt Board Story Sets, 199
Morning, Afternoon & Evening, 149
Sing a Story, 82
Story Cards, 55
Story Switcheroo, 145
Watching Beans Grow, 155
What the Sunday Funnies Really Say, 57

Shape Recognition
Circle Search, 160
Pretty Printed Patterns, 77
Shape Concentration, 114
What Can Shapes Make?, 148

Small Motor
Deep Dirt Digging, 220
Foil and Foam Sculpture, 214
Go Tiny Toe Ball Go, 213
Holey Lacies, 78
Pound, Push, Pull, and Punch Playdough, 233
Sandbox Toys and Play, 218
Snip & Cut, 216
Tiny Tapping, 227
Wet and Wild, 221
Woodworking, 228

Small Muscles. See Small Motor

Sorting
Button Sort, 135
Color Sort, 152
Nature Collection, 41
Sprigs and Twigs, 157
Take Stock of a Rock, 38
Vehicle Tally, 167

Spatial Concepts
Hooping It Up, 215
Loop-de-Loop Ball, 225
Mailing Tubes and Balls, 224
Over, Under, Around, and Through, 126
Train Engines and Cardboard Boxcars, 224

Speaking
Back-to-Back Pictures, 136
Building Together Apart, 127
What's Happening Here?, 122
Where Is It?, 113

Symbolic Thinking
Can You See My Face?, 93

T Tactile Experiences
Foot Painting, 84
Imaginary Snow, 55
Touching the Outside, 118

Testing
Bumping, Bouncing Balls, 16
Meltdown, 14
Paper Caper, 21
Rolling, Rolling, Rolling, 19
Roll Poll, 112
Weigh Away, 42
Wheel Along, 88
Where Is It?, 113
Who Fits What?, 14
Wind Detective, 177

V Visual Memory
Shape Concentration, 114

Visual Perception
Building Big Blocks for Big Block Buildings, 58

W Weighing
Weigh Away, 42

Word Recognition
Say It in a Letter, 183
Word Search, 179